Teach Now! Sci

C000200996

The companion website for this series can
www.routledge.com/cw/teachnow. All of the useful web
links highlighted in the book can be found here, along with
additional resources and activities.

Being taught by a great teacher is one of the great privileges of life.
Teach Now! *is an exciting new series that opens up the secrets of*
great teachers and, step by step, helps trainees to build the skills and
confidence they need to become first-rate classroom practitioners.

Written by a highly skilled practitioner, this practical, classroom-
focused guide contains all the support you need to become a great
science teacher. Combining a grounded, modern rationale for
learning and teaching with highly practical training approaches,
the book guides you through all the different aspects of science
teaching, offering clear, straightforward advice on classroom practice, lesson planning and working in schools.

Teaching and learning, planning, assessment and behaviour
management are all covered in detail, with a host of carefully
chosen examples used to demonstrate good practice. There are
also chapters on organising practical work, the science curriculum,
key ideas that underpin science as a subject and finding the right
job. Throughout the book, there is a wide selection of ready-to-use
activities, strategies and techniques to help you bring science alive
in all three main disciplines, including common experiments and
demonstrations from biology, physics and chemistry, to engage and
inspire you and your students.

Celebrating the whole process of engaging young people with
the awe and wonder of science, this book is your essential guide
as you start your exciting and rewarding career as an outstanding
science teacher.

Tom Sherrington has been Head Teacher at King Edward VI Grammar School in Chelmsford for several years. He is moving on to become Head Teacher at Highbury Grove School in Islington, UK, and remains a practising science teacher. His blog, headguruteacher.com, has a very wide following, and he is a regular contributor to teacher training events around the country.

Teach Now!

Series editor: Geoff Barton

Being taught by a great teacher is one of the great privileges of life. *Teach Now!* is an exciting new series that opens up the secrets of great teachers and, step-by-step, helps trainees to build the skills and confidence they need to become first-rate classroom practitioners. The series comprises a core text that explores what every teacher needs to know about essential issues such as learning, pedagogy, assessment and behaviour management, and subject specific books that guide the reader through the key components and challenges in teaching individual subjects. Written by expert practitioners, the books in this series combine an underpinning philosophy of teaching and learning alongside engaging activities, strategies and techniques to ensure success in the classroom.

Titles in the series:

Teach Now! The Essentials of Teaching
Geoff Barton

Teach Now! History
Becoming a Great History Teacher
Mike Gershon

Teach Now! English
Becoming a Great English Teacher
Alex Quigley

Teach Now! Science
The Joy of Teaching Science
Tom Sherrington

Teach Now! Modern Foreign Languages
Becoming a Great Teacher of Modern Foreign Languages
Sally Allan

Teach Now! Mathematics
Becoming a Great Mathematics Teacher
Julia Upton

Teach Now!
Science

The Joy of
Teaching Science

Tom Sherrington

Routledge
Taylor & Francis Group

LONDON AND NEW YORK

First published 2014
by Routledge
2 Park Square, Milton Park, Abingdon, Oxon OX14 4RN

and by Routledge
711 Third Avenue, New York, NY 10017

Routledge is an imprint of the Taylor & Francis Group, an informa business

British Library Cataloguing in Publication Data
A catalogue record for this book is available from the British Library

Library of Congress Cataloging in Publication Data
Sherrington, Tom.
  Teach now! science: the joy of teaching science/Tom Sherrington.
  pages cm
  1. Science – Study and teaching (Elementary) 2. Science – Study and
  teaching (Secondary) 3. Inquiry-based learning. 4. Effective teaching.
  I. Title.
  LB1585.S47 2014
  372.35'044 – dc23
  2013050710

ISBN: 978-0-415-72689-4 (hbk)
ISBN: 978-0-415-72690-0 (pbk)
ISBN: 978-1-315-76792-5 (ebk)

Typeset in Celeste and Optima
by Florence Production Ltd, Stoodleigh, Devon, UK

For Deb, Daisy and Sam

Contents

Series editor's foreword		xi
Acknowledgements		xvii
1	The joy of teaching science	1
2	How science works	15
3	The science curriculum	31
4	Planning for differentiation	51
5	Managing behaviour and building relationships	77
6	Classic teaching modes	102
7	Science as a practical subject	140
8	Formative assessment	174
9	Getting your first job	195
Bibliography		205
Index		207

Series editor's foreword

What is this series about and who is it for?

Many of us unashamedly like being teachers.

We shrug off the jibes about being in it for the holidays. We ignore the stereotypes in soap operas, sitcoms, bad films and serious news programmes. We don't feel any need to apologise for what we do, despite a constant and corrosive sense of being undervalued.

We always knew that being criticised was part of the deal.

We aren't defensive. We aren't apologetic. We simply like teaching.

And whether we still spend the majority of our working week in the classroom or, as senior leaders, we regard the classroom as a sanctuary from the swirling madness beyond the school gates, we think teaching matters.

We think it matters a lot.

And we think that students need more good teachers.

That's where 'Teach Now!' started as a concept. Could we – as a group of teachers and teaching leaders, scattered across England – put together the kind of books we wish we had had when we were embarking on our own journeys into the secret garden of education.

Of course, there were lots of books around then. Nowadays there are even more – books, plus ebooks, blogs and tweets. You can hardly move on the Internet without tripping over another reflection on a lesson that went well or badly, another teacher extolling a particular approach or dismissing another craze or moaning about the management.

So we know you don't necessarily think you need us. There's plenty of people out there ready to shovel advice and guidance towards a fledgling teacher.

But we wanted to do something different. We wanted to provide two essential texts that would distil our collective knowledge as teachers and package it in a form which was easy to read, authoritative, re-readable, reassuring and deeply rooted in the day-to-day realities of education as it is – not as a consultant or adviser might depict it.

We are writing, in other words, in the early hours of days when each of us will be teaching classes, taking assemblies, watching lessons, looking at schemes of work and dealing with naughty students – and possibly naughty teachers.

We believe this gives our series a distinctive sense of being grounded in the realities of real schools, the kind of places we each work in every day.

We want to provide a warts-and-all account of how to be a great teacher, but we also each believe that education is an essentially optimistic career.

However grim the news out there, in our classrooms we can weave a kind of magic, given the right conditions and the right behaviour. We can reassure ourselves and the students in front of us that, together, we can make the world better.

And if that seems far-fetched, then you haven't seen enough great teachers.

As Roy Blatchford – himself an exceptional teacher and now the Director of the National Education Trust – says in his list of what great teachers do:

> The best teachers are children at heart
> Sitting in the best lessons, you just don't want to leave.
> (Roy Blatchford, *The 2012 Teachers' Standards in the Classroom*, Sage, 2013)

We want young people to experience more lessons like that – classrooms where the sense of time is different, where it expands and shrinks as the world beyond the classroom recedes and where interest and passion and fascination take over; places where whatever your background your brain will fire with new experiences, thoughts and ideas; where whatever your experience so far of the adult world, here, in this classroom, is an adult who cares a lot about something, can communicate it vividly and, in the way she or he talks and behaves, demonstrates a care and interest in you that is remarkable.

We need more classrooms like that and more teachers to take their place within them.

So that's what we have set out to do: to create a series of books that will – if you share our sense of moral purpose – help you to become a great teacher.

You'll have noticed that we expect you to buy two books. We said we were optimistic. That's because we think that being a great teacher has two important dimensions to it. First, you need to know your subject – to really know it.

We know from very good sources that the most effective teachers are experts in what they teach. That doesn't mean they know everything about it. In fact, they often fret about how little they feel they truly know. But they are hungry and passionate and eager – and all those other characteristics that define the teachers who inspire us.

So we know that subject knowledge is really important – and not just for teaching older students. It is as important when teaching Year 7s, knowing what you need to teach and what you can, for now, ignore.

We also believe that subject knowledge is much more than a superficial whisk through key dates or key concepts. It's about having a depth of knowledge that allows us to join up ideas, to explore complexity and nuance, to make decisions about what the key building-blocks of learning a subject might be.

Great teachers sense this and, over a number of years, they build their experience and hone their skills. That's why we have developed subject specialist books for English, mathematics, history, modern foreign languages and science. These are the books that will help you to take what you learnt on your degree course and to think through how to make that knowledge and those skills powerfully effective in the classroom.

They will take you from principles to practice, from philosophy deep into pedagogy. They will help to show you that any terror you may have about becoming a teacher of a subject is inevitable, and that knowing your stuff, careful planning, informed strategies – that all of these will help you to teach now.

Then there's *Teach Now! The Essentials of Teaching*, which is the core text because we also believe that even if you are the best informed scientist, linguist or mathematician in the universe, that this in itself won't make you a great teacher.

That's because great teachers do things that support and supplement their subject knowledge. This is the stuff that the late, great educator Michael Marland called the 'craft of the classroom'. It's what the best teachers know and do instinctively but, to those of us looking on from the outside, or in the earliest stages of a teaching career, can seem mysterious, unattainable, a kind of magic.

It's also the kind of stuff that conventional training may not sufficiently cover.

We're talking about how to open the classroom door, knowing where to stand, knowing what to say to the student who is cheeky, knowing how to survive when you feel, in the darkest of glooms, intimidated by preparation and by marking, that you have made a terrible career choice.

These two texts combined – the subject specialist book and the core book – are designed to help you wherever you are training – in a school or academy or on a PGCE course. Whether you are receiving expert guidance, or it's proving to be more mixed, we hope our ideas, approaches and advice will reassure you, and help you to gain in confidence.

We hope we are providing books that you will want to read and re-read as you train, as you take up your first post and as you finally shrug off the feelings of early insecurity and start to stretch your wings as a fully fledged teacher.

So that's the idea behind the books.

And throughout the writing of them we have been very conscious that – just like us – you have too little time. We have therefore aimed to write in a style that is easy-to-read, reassuring, occasionally provocative and opinionated. We don't want to be bland: teaching is too important for any of us to wilt under a weight of colourless eduspeak.

That's why we have written in short paragraphs, short chapters, added occasional points for reflection and discussion, comments from trainee and veteran teachers, and aimed throughout to create practical, working guides to help you teach now.

So thanks for choosing to read what we have provided. We would love to hear how your early journey into teaching goes and hope that our series helps you on your way into and through a rewarding and enjoyable career.

Geoff Barton
with Sally Allan, Mike Gershon, Alex Quigley, Tom Sherrington and Julia Upton
The *Teach Now!* team of authors

Acknowledgements

I'd like to thank Geoff Barton for asking me to join him in producing this series. His guidance on the early chapters helped me enormously, with comments that were sharp, constructive and encouraging in equal measure. For a first-time writer, it was a real privilege receiving Geoff's detailed feedback. I'm also indebted to Alex Quigley, author of the English counterpart to this book. Our frequent exchanges helped a great deal, as the ideas for the book took shape.

I'm very grateful for the input of my colleagues at King Edward VI Grammar School. Kirsten Smith, Sandra Naish and David Hall have helped by contributing ideas for science experiments; Bill Wheeler gave useful advice about the philosophy of science section. Technicians Peter Oxford, Barbara Basso-Bert and Paul Strudwick have supported me superbly in my teaching at KEGS, and the sections on science as a practical subject owe a great deal to them.

Finally, I would like to thank my wife, fellow science teacher and school leader, Deb O'Connor. We've shared our life as science teachers for over twenty years, living and breathing our passion for teaching. Many of the ideas in this book have developed from our discussions. My hope is that the *Teach Now!* series goes some way to helping new teachers become as effective and inspiring as she is.

Tom Sherrington
December 2013

1 The joy of teaching science

I love teaching; I love being a teacher; I love working in schools. I especially love teaching science.

I initially entered the profession with some trepidation, unsure of where it would lead, but it has proven to be a highly rewarding occupation, offering boundless opportunities for personal development and enjoyment. I've found that teaching science can be, in turn, intellectually stimulating, creative, experimental and highly rewarding in terms of developing relationships with students.

It's just wonderful to be the one who gets to introduce a class of young people to the idea of natural selection and reveal the extraordinary story of evolution; or to excite students by making their hair stand on end with a Van der Graaf generator, bringing the theory behind electricity off the page; or to be the person who makes the carbon ooze out of a flask of sugar with concentrated sulphuric acid to show how extraordinary chemical reactions can be.

There really is no job quite like it. Of course, it isn't always easy; in fact, sometimes it can be really tough. But, with the right spirit and the right tools, for the most part, the rewards are enormous, and teaching science is a great joy.

Teaching is also learning

A recurring theme in this book is that the ideas that make up the subject of science are at the heart of the joy of teaching it. I have found, over the years, that teaching has deepened my understanding and my passion for science, often in ways that have surprised me. In my own specialist area, physics, I have learned so much about gravity, waves and fundamental particles through teaching. As a general science teacher for many years, I've had to learn a lot more about genetics and evolution than I'd covered in my biology O level, and, in chemistry, I now have a much more sophisticated understanding of the link between chemical structures and material properties and the range of chemical reactions that can be performed in a school laboratory.

The process of continuing to learn the subject is a passion that most science teachers share. For example, at a recent physics department meeting at my school, we were trying out some new experiments to show our students.

One was a slow-motion camera that could shoot 1,000 frames per second. We used it to film a balloon filled with water at the moment of its being burst with a pin. The result was fabulous to see: the rubber balloon parts flew off, leaving the water in a completely formed balloon shape, before, eventually, it fell apart. This illustration of intermolecular forces in water was fascinating, fun to produce and completely new to me.

We also looked at a large-scale capacitor made from two layers of unrolled aluminium foil, about 1 m long, separated by a thin plastic sheet and attached to a high-tension (5 kV) supply. The result was a series of high-voltage discharges through the plastic, accompanied by some impressively loud bangs. In my subsequent lessons, the students found these demonstrations extremely engaging: they generated a wide range of interesting questions, and we all learned something and had fun in the process. For me, this is the joy of teaching science, and I hope it will be for you too.

The learning obviously isn't confined to the content of the subject; it is also the professional learning that goes with being a teacher. Over time, new pedagogical ideas emerge; there are all kinds of fads and trends and new directives, but, even without all of the circus hoop jumping that goes on in schools, there are still so many different ways to explain ideas and to make connections between theory and practice.

As the book develops, I hope you will be able to explore your own ideas about some of the fundamental concepts in science and how they all fit together, in some kind of order that will allow you to make sense of it for your students.

It is likely that any group of science teachers in a school will have arrived via different routes, with different degrees and science specialisms. Depending on your school's structure and philosophy, it may be that you only teach physics, chemistry or biology. Certainly, it is very common for teachers to teach just one of these subjects to A level; it is also very common up to GCSE. However, at Key Stage 3 (KS3) and very often at GCSE, teachers are expected to share the teaching of science, irrespective of their degree specialisms.

I have argued in the past that a strong general science teacher is far more use to a student than a weaker specialist. However, subject knowledge certainly does make a difference in drilling down to the deeper concepts at the highest attainment levels. In writing this book, I am going to attempt to strike a balance by addressing issues relevant to all teachers of science in general, with examples and specific ideas from physics, chemistry and biology woven in.

To get you thinking about what you know, here are some questions. Think about what a one-line answer would be, and then what a 'four mark' answer might be. Go deeper and deeper – asking 'why?' – until you just don't know:

- Why do magnets attract or repel each other?

- Why does your heart beat faster during exercise?

- How does a rainbow work? And what about a mirage? What is that?

The joy of teaching science

- What exactly does double-glazing do?
- Why is a hypothermia blanket shiny on both sides?
- Why is diesel fuel less flammable than petrol but doesn't need a spark plug to ignite?
- Is it true that whales and hippos are closely related? How is this possible?
- Why are spiders so clever, the way they spin those webs? (Trick question)
- How do we get iron from rocks?
- Why do we bend our knees when jumping down from a wall?
- How do plants know what the seasons are?
- Why do astronauts seem weightless in a space station, when they are still in orbit?
- How far is it to the next nearest galaxy? How do we know?
- Why is graphene so flexible and strong, when it is only one molecule thick?
- Which way do the electrons move in a bolt of lightning?
- What is fire? Exactly . . .
- Why is potassium metal so reactive in water?

ACTIVITIES

If you are unsure about any of these answers, do some research, talk to colleagues in your school and develop your own scientific knowledge and understanding. It is so much easier to teach a topic where you feel really confident in the subject matter.

All science teachers have areas of relative strength and lots of gaps. Work out what your gaps are and start to fill them!

Science is all about posing good questions and searching for the answers.

Scientific thinking: thinking like a scientist

Another of the pleasures of teaching science is the opportunity to engage with the 'real' science community, past and present, both experimental and theoretical, involving students in the process of thinking like a scientist.

This takes many forms. At a basic level, there is the 'how stuff works' dimension: this applies to the properties of everyday materials and machines, cooking food, plant responses, diseases, teeth, ears, the heart, magnets, motors and the weather. How do they work, and how do we know that?

Then there is the 'fundamental truth' dimension – the big existential questions. How did life on Earth develop? How are living things connected, and how has that changed over time? What is energy, what is matter made of, and how does it all hold together? How can we get a sense of the scale of the subatomic world and of the universe, both in space and in time, and how does the living world interact with the physical world that it inhabits?

Of course, then we have the measurement and verification dimension. How do we construct experiments that allow us to measure variables in a controlled, systematic fashion, such that our analysis can lead to valid conclusions? Having the opportunity to work through all of these questions with a class of young people is wonderful.

The traditional and modern scientific approaches that have been employed over time are a constant reference point for gaining a perspective on the development of scientific ideas. The personal triumphs, disasters and accidental discoveries by scientific figures offer a dimension to the study of science that really helps to bring it alive. Whether we're talking about Galileo and the great 'ball drop' experiment, the painstaking work of Darwin and Wallace in arriving at the idea of natural selection, the arrangement of the elements by Dmitri Mendeleev, or more recent breakthroughs with the human genome and the Higgs boson, the people are part of the story, alongside their discoveries and ideas.

Of course, one of the great assets to teachers of science faced with a cohort of teenagers immersed in social media and the latest technology is that our subject is continually being updated. Science is simultaneously timeless and cutting edge. Scientific ideas are in the news every week, and a great science teacher will find ways to weave the newest events and breakthroughs into the curriculum, to keep it alive, fresh and of the moment. Science doesn't stand still.

Science is multidisciplinary

For a lot of science teachers, one of the greatest joys is the massive variety of activities that you can engage in during lessons. Although there is a lot of time spent with theoretical concepts, thinking and writing answers to problems and performing calculations, much as you might do in many other subjects, science is also a practical subject, with a major 'hands-on' element.

As we will discuss later, it is really important to know how the practical work and theory work together – not all experiments help to explain basic concepts; they can actually make things a lot more confusing, because real life is messy. However, very often, the practical lessons and demonstrations are the best bits – and are certainly the things students remember long afterwards. As a science teacher, you have the opportunity to create some big bangs and blows – igniting the perfect oxygen–hydrogen mix in a balloon or methane bubbles in detergent; you can experience the messy but fascinating process of dissecting an eye, a heart or a set of sheep lungs; and, my personal favourites, you get to make motors and create all kinds of mischief with sound and light.

At a fundamental level, scientific thinking is all about matching theory with experiment, and we have ample opportunity to do this in the school laboratory. We can tell the story of our understanding of light as a wave and a particle and the development of our knowledge of fundamental particles through the perspective of the history of ideas needing experimental verification and experimental discoveries looking for a theoretical underpinning. This applies to the story of natural selection and genetics and our observations of materials in all their glorious diversity, despite being made up of only a few common building blocks.

Of course, science is also an academic discipline that requires us to use research skills, to have the power to write explanations in good English and to produce an analysis of data using graphs and calculations. As teachers, these elements of the role are really important, not least because these skills are those that are relied on heavily during formal exams. Mainly, we need them to share our ideas within the class. There is a level of rigour required – accuracy and precision – alongside a certain flair and imagination.

We need to develop skills for using a range of weird and wonderful apparatus, and this takes time to master. From simple clocks, ammeters and voltmeters to baffling oscilloscopes, tricky microscopes and fiddly bits of glassware, there is a lot to learn. However, with technicians and teacher colleagues to support you, it soon becomes one of the pleasures of the job. Every year that I've been a science teacher, I've learned something new about a piece of kit or I've found a new way to measure something.

So, a science teacher needs to be a thinker, a mathematician, a writer, a technician, a storyteller, a historian – a veritable polymath. If you've never thought of yourself as a multitasker, you're about to be amazed.

Autonomy

Teaching wouldn't be fun at all if every lesson was prescribed, and you had to do exactly what you were told by someone else. We haven't come this far just to be vehicles for transmitting information. We're here to engage our students in a rigorous learning process, but also to make sure we are getting a lot out of it too. The more motivated and enthusiastic you are as a teacher, the more likely you are to transmit those things to your students and to sustain yourself as a professional when things get tough. In this context, teaching science is brilliant, because, to a large extent, you have a high degree of autonomy.

Of course, there is a syllabus – and we will deal with planning a curriculum later. But, for any given idea or topic, there are hundreds of ways to organise a lesson to make things interesting and to suit your personal style.

In terms of autonomy, this means that, from day to day, you are doing what you decide to do. You might want to do a practical with all the students, or show a video clip you found, or run a demonstration. You might want students to work on their own, or to collaborate in pairs or groups; you might want them to produce a piece of extended writing or a multimedia product or simply to give extended oral presentations. You can use textbooks, some resources you have designed or borrowed or interactive online materials, or you can make up questions as part of an extended question and answer exchange.

Some methods might work better than others, and there are some important elements of pedagogy that you'll want to embed into your daily routines – aspects of formative assessment and questioning – but there are so many options, and you have the freedom to choose. If anything, the choice can be overwhelming, and, to begin with, you may start out with a solid borrowed framework that you embellish in your own way later on.

However, as many teachers will tell you, one of the aspects of the job that sustains them is the joy of closing the door and having a space where they can create whatever they want to with their students. As I always say: you don't need permission to be great!

Going off piste and being agile

Agility is the word I use to describe a key characteristic of a great teacher. It's all about the ability to adapt, to change course, to respond, to deal with multiple simultaneous demands, to keep up with all the individual students' learning needs, to be spontaneous and flexible and to think on your feet; 'thinking on your feet' is a hugely important teacher skill.

I think it is safe to say that many really good lessons don't go according to plan. Why? Because, in truth, the plan is usually highly skeletal: it is just a rough outline of where to start and where the lesson will be going in general, but the details depend on what happens next at each stage. In an environment where I am challenging my students at a high level and trying hard to tease out their individual weak spots, I'm never exactly sure how students will respond or what questions they might ask. But, as an agile teacher, I'm ready for anything.

Sometimes, agility is needed to rescue a bad situation, like a goalkeeper pouncing, but, mostly, agility is about seeking out the most engaging, most challenging path to keep the flow of learning going . . . like an off piste skier. This is the part of being a teacher that I love the most. At a basic level, a routine, probing question and answer session is a great test of agility. This is the pedagogical equivalent of sparring. Great teachers love it, taking students' statements and questions and then returning more probing responses. With whole-class response methods, the challenge is greater, and so are the rewards.

An agile teacher will take any opportunity to make connections to current developments, scrapping the planned lesson if necessary. Venus is transiting the sun, the Higgs boson has been discovered, Richard III has been found and verified with carbon dating, there has been a tsunami: all these things are a reason to go right off at a tangent and bring learning into the real world. In fact, when these things happen, it is unforgivable not to.

Students and teachers find great joy in the kind of spontaneity that allows anyone in the room to express their puzzlement, their curiosity or their sheer love of the subject at any given time. Recent diversions in my lessons have led us to consider the James May 'milk first' tea-making theory based on temperature gradient and specific heat capacity, how a bullet-proof vest works (following the input of a materials enthusiast in my A level class) and what might happen in terms of g-force if we could fly through the sun. Is it on the syllabus? Not exactly . . . but who cares?

Inspiring awe

Take a look at the image in Figure 1.1. It is the Hubble Ultra-Deep Field, photographed over several days in 2003–4. As explained by Professor Brian Cox, in this patch of sky, imagined on a scale the size of a thumbnail placed 75 feet away, there are over 10,000

Figure 1.1 The Hubble Ultra-Deep Field
Source: Image Asset Management Ltd/Alamy

objects, invisible to the naked eye. Each object is not a star but a galaxy, each with hundreds of millions of stars.

The light from some of the objects has been travelling towards us almost since the beginning of time. So, looking at the image is like looking back into time, as well as into the enormity of space. For me, this is 'awesome' in the truest sense. It fills me with *awe*.

What does this mean exactly?

- It provokes an emotional response – it is beautiful, thrilling, magnificent.

- It forces me to rethink some fundamental conceptual ideas, to update my mental model.

- It creates a sense of scale that makes me look on my small world with a new perspective.

- It raises lots of questions and makes me curious to know even more.

- It is impressive as a human discovery, a human achievement.

This is *awe* . . . often experienced alongside its counterpart *wonder*. One of the joys of teaching science is being able to step back from time to time to contemplate the subject in hand, instilling a sense of awe. This is how the seeds of a deep-rooted love of learning are sown. We're not just learning this stuff because we have to, or because it is useful. We are learning it because it is just so fabulously, fascinatingly awe-inspiring. There is no greater motivation to learn than this.

Clearly, in a five-period day, with exams to prepare for and a pile of marking to look forward to, you may feel your inclination to inspire awe may be on the low side. But who else is going to do this if we don't?

In fact, we should aim to make it our default mode, our natural disposition, to seize every possible opportunity to fire our students' imaginations and to stoke their passions. This is as important to a school's contribution to social, moral, spiritual and cultural education as any number of assemblies. Is it unrealistic to think of inspiring awe as a habit for any teacher? I don't think so – and, as science teachers, we certainly have plenty of material.

I naturally feel that most of our subject is awe-inspiring. Playing with a pair of magnets is a wonderful thing ... just sensing that invisible, mysterious force. Seeing a simple current-carrying wire moving in between a pair of magnets ... well that is extraordinary. Imagine Faraday's surprise and delight. The inner flower garden revealed by cutting open a fig – and the evolutionary story behind it – or, in chemistry, handling rocks that are millions of years in the making ... it is all awe-inspiring, if we just take the trouble to create that moment of wonder in our lessons.

For me, and I hope for you too, this isn't superficial stuff. Inspiring awe is a core function for teachers: it's what we should be doing. We need to take every opportunity we can to communicate our own feeling that life is full of wondrous things that are there to be studied, discovered and enjoyed.

Relationships with students

Later on we will deal with the nuts and bolts of behaviour management, but, at a fairly basic level, your capacity to enjoy being a teacher will depend to a very large extent on how much joy you take from being around teenagers. Establishing relationships can be hard work; it can be emotional and, occasionally, very personal and painful, especially with a new class, when you're still on a steep learning curve. However, it is hard to imagine enjoying teaching if you don't enjoy the process of forming these relationships.

If this already sounds daunting, don't worry. It doesn't have to be 'up close and personal'. You don't have to be anything more than a professional person doing a serious job, and schools have all manner of support systems to fall back on when you need them. It takes time to develop the confidence you need to be at ease with any class and the maturity or experience to be thick-skinned enough not to be battered by every teenage mood swing that takes the shape of a jibe in your direction. However, being around young people needs to be something you enjoy, once you've got things working the way you want them to.

When teachers look back on their work, they rarely talk about the great lesson they taught on osmosis in plant cells, or the superb scheme of work they wrote on hydrocarbons. Much more often they talk about the students they taught: the ones who made them laugh and cry; the ones who blew them away with their ideas or made a connection with them through their humour, their kindness or their dedication. Ultimately, we are not just teachers of science, we are teachers of students; the teaching and learning of science create the context for the relationships we forge. It is better to enjoy this as much as possible, as hard as it can be, because most of the time this is what makes the job worth doing.

Achievement is its own reward

In truth, there is something even better than the relationships. Joyful as it may be, forming relationships is actually a by-product of the process that is our core purpose: teaching science and creating the conditions for our students to learn and to achieve. You may teach students where your relationship has been fraught with tribulations and confrontations; you may teach students where every lesson was a giant love-in. Either way, the greatest rewards of all come when those students show you that they've got it, they've made a leap forward, the penny has dropped . . . the light bulb has gone on. Dah-da! Finally, Eureka!

When this happens, you don't need to give prizes: no stickers, stamps or house points. The joy that students experience – and that you feel in parallel, as the person who got them there – is greater than any token or reward. Achievement really is its own reward. It is also, by far, the greatest joy of teaching. All the hard work, all the sweat, the hours of preparation, the time spent giving carefully considered feedback, the inspiration and perseverance in the face of the odds, the ups and downs of forming those relationships ... all of that is paid off handsomely when students achieve, when they reach the far-away goals that you set them at the beginning. It's pure joy.

This can happen in small moments in a lesson – lots of micro-steps of progress towards a bigger goal. A student's smile as they give a great answer or hand in a great piece of work, the beaming pride a student shows when you praise them for doing something impressive that they had struggled over – these are the lovely moments that make your day and theirs and make it all worthwhile. It can also happen in a big way on exam results days – the elation of securing achievement: there is nothing like it.

As we go through the rest of this book, the theme of 'joy' will resurface. Most of the chapters are very practical, grounded in the reality of daily school life, but hopefully, you will engage with the ideas with a certain spirit that gives you more than just professional satisfaction. Teaching great science lessons is not just our professional responsibility; it is the most rewarding job I can think of. Teaching great lessons is a joy and a great, great privilege. So, let's get started ...

TALKING POINTS

1 What is it about being a science teacher that you are most excited by or daunted by?
2 Which areas of science do you feel you need to explore much further to give you real confidence in the classroom?
3 Which ideas or phenomena in science are the ones you're really looking forward to sharing with the students in your classes?

2 How science works

When my son started secondary school, his very first homework was from his science teacher. It began with an explanation of the ideas of the Greek philosopher Democritus, who observed that water behaved in similar ways to sand – it could be stirred, poured and mixed. His hypothesis was that water might, therefore, be made up of small particles, akin to grains of sand, but smaller than the eye can see. He called these particles *atoma*.

The questions that followed were:

- What is the difference between science and philosophy?
- What observations did Democritus make?
- What was his hypothesis?
- What properties of liquids could be explained by Democritus' hypothesis?
- Does his hypothesis explain the behaviour of solids and gases?

I thought this was a fabulous way to start off a science education at secondary school: big, fundamental questions from the beginning and some key ideas about how science works.

While tackling this homework, my son asked: 'Are atoms solids on their own? Would that mean liquids are really made of solids?' He knew this wasn't right, but he was exploring his own mental model. His teacher had got him off to a flying start, thinking about

15

science, exploring ideas he'd never thought of and working out how to build up models of the physical world in ways that make sense.

To be a great science teacher, it is important to have a good understanding of the principles that underpin the subject, so that you can generate discussions like this. A good grounding in the philosophy and history of science will help you to ask good probing questions, to help make the links between experiments and theories and to reinforce recurring ideas about evidence, measurement and uncertainty.

Basic philosophy of science

It's possible to dive into teaching science by focusing on facts, models and experiments in a straightforward, unquestioning manner. However, it pays dividends for you and your students to make some of our assumptions explicit.

- What do we mean by the idea of a 'fact'?
- What do we mean when we talk about 'proof' or 'theory'?
- Are we teaching a set of neutral, objective truths, or are we teaching collections of ideas that only hold true within our own specific sociocultural framework?

If you've never studied this area formally, I highly recommend reading *Philosophy of Science: A Very Short Introduction*, by Samir Okasha (2002). This short book gives a superb, concise overview of the key questions. Some ideas that are fascinating to consider include:

- **The idea of inductive reasoning** as a sound procedure and the assumption of universal physical laws – what David Hume called the 'uniformity of nature': In everyday science, we assume that a phenomenon that occurs every time we observe will continue to occur in a predictable manner. We assume that the laws of science will work in every area of space and at every time in the same way. Hume was critical of this assumption. It's a fascinating philosophical question.

- **Karl Popper**'s ideas about deductive reasoning and the notion that scientific theories must be falsifiable: for Popper, areas of study that cannot be subjected to this test – such as Freudian and Marxist theories – cannot be considered as a science.

- **Thomas Kuhn**'s idea of scientific revolutions and the concept of 'paradigm shift': Here, the idea is that our understanding of nature undergoes major changes over time, as exemplified by the revolutions in scientific thinking inspired by Copernicus, Darwin and Einstein. Crucially, according to Kuhn, most scientists accept the validity of the prevailing paradigm to a high degree; they don't question it. They work within the confines of the paradigm, tweaking the rules to explain certain experimental results. According to Kuhn, it requires a large accumulation of anomalous results for a paradigm shift to occur and for enough people to accept the new thinking. In this sense, there is a degree of subjective reasoning at play and a degree of peer pressure among members of the scientific community. Kuhn was suggesting that science isn't based on rational thought alone.

These are all big questions – and there are many more. A science curriculum that is rich in big questions about life, time, space and matter and the scientific process itself is what you should aim to deliver. Clearly, scientific understanding is much more than a set of fixed ideas and principles; it is a dynamic collection of theories and concepts that change continually.

Nevertheless, with all that said, as a science teacher, it is perfectly possible to teach day to day without ever having engaged with the subject's philosophical underpinning. You can go a long way just telling your students that everything in the curriculum is a fact based on the evidence we have accumulated to date.

In practice, our main goal in teaching science is to help our students to understand the concepts and phenomena in physics, chemistry and biology as they are generally understood. If we want them to get to grips with the ideas, there is great value in keeping things simple. The philosophical questions can sit in the background while you demonstrate and explain ideas on the basis that they are true.

For example, many biological processes involve complex sequences of chemical reactions, with subtle concentration gradients and multiple variables. However, we usually teach about photosynthesis and respiration at a simplified level, as if they are isolated reactions. In a lot of physics questions, we take out complex sources of friction, heat loss or electrical resistance, to allow students to access the core principles of mechanics, energy and electricity.

This is entirely legitimate. If you are explicit about the fact that real-world problems are more complicated, you can teach the basic models as being factually accurate. That builds confidence and gives coherence to the ideas, as they link across the curriculum. Gradually, as students develop their understanding, you can peel back more layers to reveal deeper levels of complexity.

The classic approach of modern science, originated by Galileo, is to look for a coherent set of models based on evidence. The accepted, modern scientific method that is reinforced across the curriculum is basically this:

- Observations and measurements are made to establish relationships between variables.

- These relationships lead to the formulation of hypotheses about underlying mechanisms and structures.

- Hypotheses are then used to make predictions that can be tested by experiments.

- Hypotheses that make successful predictions consistently become accepted as theories.

Of course, there are lots of examples of accidental discoveries (such as with the discovery of penicillin) and plenty of examples of theoretical predictions that are later verified by experiment.

The interplay of theory and experiment is at the heart of what makes science so fascinating, not only for what it tells us about the world around us, but also for what it reveals about the human desire for knowledge and our determination to seek out the truth.

Ideas from the history of science

There are many ideas in science that you can bring to life for students by telling the story of how they developed over time.

The solar system and cosmology

A superb example is the story of **Copernicus** and **Galileo** and how they revolutionised our understanding of the solar system. Their work established the idea of the heliocentric system, at great cost to themselves. Galileo was able to make observations that verified the hypothesis put forward by Copernicus, but the Catholic Church treated both with contempt and suspicion.

The Copernican heliocentric model explains the motions of the planets in a more complete way than the previous geocentric model, and, consequently, despite fierce resistance from religious institutions, the idea became accepted. Newton's universal law of gravitation, which involved the invention of modern calculus, seemed to represent a complete model of the motion of stars and planets. However, Einstein's ideas of general and special relativity and Hubble's evidence for an expanding universe added another level of complexity.

The sequence of these ideas as conceptual models matches their development over time. It also matches developments in technology that allowed more sophisticated measurements to be undertaken to verify the theoretical ideas.

Light: wave or particle?

The story of how we know what we know about the nature of light is fascinating. Starting with Newton's 'corpuscular model', reflection and refraction can be explained reasonably well. However, diffraction and interference cannot.

The wave model of light, supported by Huygens' theory, could explain these phenomena, but it took over a century before the famous Young's double slit experiment showed that light exhibited very clear, wave-like properties. The emergence of sufficiently coherent light sources made this possible. Another century later, and the problem of the photoelectric effect challenged the wave model. Shining light on to plates in a circuit revealed effects that couldn't be accounted for, unless the light was both wave-like and particle-like, simultaneously. This led Einstein to propose the idea of wave-particle duality, building on Planck's idea of quantised energy.

Again, the historical development of our understanding helps provide a logical sequence through the topic, allowing students to build up a conceptual model. They also learn that ideas have to be able to withstand challenges over time, if they are to survive as fundamental theories about our natural world.

Evolution and genetics

As is often stated, the theory of evolution is one of mankind's greatest achievements. The stories of Charles Darwin and Alfred Wallace are extraordinary. Their journeys to examine plant and animal species from around the world are epic tales of heroic adventure. The conclusions they came to, based on their observations of adaptations of species in niche habitats, were massively significant and will remain so for all time.

The idea of non-random natural selection as a process by which all living things have evolved over time is one of the most exciting to teach and to learn. Richard Dawkins' *The Greatest Show on Earth* (2009) set out the ideas behind evolution brilliantly. His book *The Ancestor's Tale* (2005) is one of my favourite science books. Here, he moves back through time, describing, in a magnificent style, how different species originate from common ancestors.

The discovery of genetic material in every cell and the idea of heredity weave beautifully into the evolution story. This encompasses Mendel's experiments with pea plants, later leading to our understanding of dominant and recessive genes. It then leads to the discovery of the structure of DNA by Watson and Crick and more recent explorations into GM crops, laboratory-grown beef burgers and the continuing successes of genome mapping.

The evidence for evolution also draws in various other scientific areas. Estimates of the age of the universe determined from cosmology and radioactive dating of rocks have provided evidence for the age of the Earth. At 4.5 billion years, we know the Earth is old enough for evolutionary processes to have led us from primitive life forms on slimy hot rocks to the abundance of life we know now.

Processes such as X-ray crystallography enabled Rosalind Franklin to propose the double helix structure for DNA that was later verified by Watson and Crick. The evidence from patterns of magnetism on the mid Atlantic ocean floor supports the theory of plate tectonics, which in turn explains patterns of divergence among species on continents around the world.

All of these ideas reinforce our understanding of, and confidence in, the theory of evolution. With a well-structured curriculum, the story of evolution can be told repeatedly, in greater depth as each of these ideas comes forward.

Elements, atoms and fundamental particles

Returning to my son's science homework, ever since Democritus, scientists have been trying to explain how the phenomena we observe can be explained in terms of the behaviour of fundamental particles. The development of the periodic table, including Mendeleev's ideas of periodicity, is a wonderful way to bring chemistry alive.

Marie Curie's story, exploring the phenomenon she called *radioactivity* and ending with her death from the effects of radiation exposure, helps to put the early observations into a historical context. The development of the Bohr model of the atom, after Rutherford's famous alpha-scattering experiment and the subsequent growth of particle and quantum physics spearheaded by Einstein, Schrödinger and Dirac, is like a walk through the concepts.

The story ends in the present with all the work that is going on at the Large Hadron Collider at CERN in Geneva. It's very exciting to have contemporary science to report on, but it makes a lot more sense if students know how the story began.

'Quantum', Einstein, Bohr and the Great Debate about the Nature of Reality, by Manjit Kumar, tells the whole story superbly well. Einstein believed that quantum models were not a description of physical reality; Bohr believed that they were, and it turns out that Einstein was wrong!

There are three other books I recommend that you read to gain a broad overview of the background to science. They are especially helpful if you are trying to develop your knowledge in non-specialist areas, but, even for an expert, they are a wonderful read:

- *A Short History of Nearly Everything*, by Bill Bryson (2010).
- *The Faber Book of Science*, edited by John Carey (1995).
- *The Oxford Book of Modern Science Writing*, edited by Richard Dawkins (2008).

ACTIVITIES

Consider the examples given here and think about your own knowledge of the details in each one. Take some time to explore them in more depth.

Think about other, similar historical developments that you could add as further examples and look to see where they could help to provide extra depth and context in your teaching.

Experimental method

A key aspect of teaching science is ensuring that students develop the skills and understanding needed to design, carry out and interpret experiments.

Early on, it is important for students to understand the key concepts of **dependent and independent variables**; sometimes, these are referred to as input and outcome variables. The idea of a **fair test**, where only one variable is changed at a time, has to be reinforced many times, alongside the idea of **control variables**: which things are we going to keep the same? Variables are then linked by **relationships**.

An example of how to teach these ideas is to find out which features of a pipe determine the frequency of the sound. Is it the width? Is it the material? Is it the length?

Give Year 7 students a selection of pipes made of glass, plastic and metal, cut to different fixed lengths and with different set widths. Their task is to design a fair test. They need to compare two pipes where only one variable is different, to determine whether the note changes when they blow down the pipe. Eventually, they work out that only the length changes the note.

This example, among others, was part of the King's College Cognitive Acceleration through Science Education programme, which provided a set of incrementally more difficult activities to force students to think in different ways about scientific processes.

It is important to show students that variables have relationships in many forms:

- Linear relationships: extension of a spring with mass.
- Null relationships: period of oscillation of a pendulum with mass (the mass cancels).
- Limiting relationships: rate of photosynthesis with increasing light levels.
- Complex non-linear relationships: rate of reaction with increasing temperature.

- Optimum conditions relationships: Haber process or enzyme function with temperature.

- Reciprocal relationship: gas pressure with volume.

- Interacting relationships over time: predator–prey populations over time.

Further thinking is needed to establish whether relationships are causal, due to association with a separate third variable or are simply disconnected chance correlations. There are also aspects of science, particularly in relation to human behaviour, where the data is more subjective and need to be analysed for bias.

The design of experiments is dictated partly by the need to control variables, but also by the need for accurate results that people will trust. This is a central issue in the science curriculum.

The Language of Measurement: Terminology Used in School Science Investigations (Association for Science Education, 2010) contains definitions of a range of concepts that underpin modern science experiments:

- error
- accuracy
- precision
- resolution
- validity
- repeatability
- reproducibility
- hypothesis
- prediction.

These terms are often incorporated into GCSE assessments, and so it is worthwhile knowing the precise definitions and using them in the classroom or laboratory. Some useful examples include:

- *Using a ruler to measure the length of a table*: you can't simply measure the table over and over again to get a more precise result; you would need a measuring device with higher resolution.

- *Throwing arrows at the bullseye on a dartboard*: darts clustered together but gathered away from the centre are precise but inaccurate (see Figure 2.1). Darts that are spread but, on average, are centred on the bullseye could be accurate but not precise (see Figure 2.2).

- *Measuring the energy released by burning crisps to heat water*: heat loss to the environment is so large that the experiment, although repeatable, is not necessarily valid, given the error in assuming that all the crisps' energy transfers to the water.

- *Using five people with five stop-clocks to measure the time for a runner to complete 100 m*: each clock has the same resolution. There are systematic timing errors owing to reaction times. An average of all five clocks would produce a more valid, more accurate answer than one clock on its own. However, we can't obtain an answer that is more precise than the clock resolutions or spread of results allow.

- *Plant growth experiments* throw up the issue of hidden variables. A tray of identical seeds grown in what appear to be identical conditions will still show variation. Of course, the seeds are not identical, and, at a cellular level, neither are the conditions. Here, there is a need to introduce the idea of sample size and a statistical evaluation of the results in order to establish meaningful relationships between variables.

Teaching students to recognise the limitations to scientific evidence is as important as showing them how to obtain it, and this should form a key part of the discussion during practicals and demonstrations.

Figure 2.1 Precision

Figure 2.2 Accuracy

> **ACTIVITY**
>
> Look up the Association for Science Education's *The Language of Measurement* (2010). Check your understanding of each of the terms and think of a practical example to illustrate each one.

Facts, beliefs and opinions

There are a number of topics in science where you may find you need to make a judgement as to how to accommodate your students' opinions, biases and religious beliefs. Your response needs to be consistent with your school policy, but, perhaps most importantly, it needs to reflect a sound application of scientific principles.

Creationism or 'intelligent design'

This is quite straightforward. Evolution is a fact. It is a theory that is supported by many layers of evidence and it can make successful predictions. It is as secure a theory as almost any other we have in science. Creationism, as we all know, has no basis in science, but is promoted through religious conviction; it's a kind of science denial.

Confronted with a creationist student or parent, try to avoid engaging in a debate. Never fall into the trap of allowing creationism and evolution to be presented as equally valid alternative theories; no self-respecting science teacher should do this. It is quite possible to stick to the facts without engaging in a theological discussion. At the same time, remember that most religious people are not creationists; it's important to challenge that misconception if it arises.

At my school, at every prospective parents' evening I say: 'We teach that evolution is a fact, because it is'. In your school, you may need to make that case yourself.

Sex education

Teaching about human reproduction is a core part of the biology curriculum. The main role of a science teacher is to teach the biological facts, whereas sex and relationships education (SRE) might be delivered by someone else. However, the two are inseparable in practice.

If you are asked questions about sexuality and gender, or abortion and contraception, it helps to be able to explain the relevant facts in a neutral manner. However, there is also a layer of information that is driven by accepted social, legal, moral and ethical conventions.

These issues should be covered by school policies, and you should be sure to follow the standard school position, rather than projecting your personal viewpoints. It is important to show an awareness of the law surrounding equalities issues, where prejudice against lesbian, gay, bisexual or transgender people has the same status as racism.

As an activity in lessons, a well-managed debate about the ethics of abortion or the role of condoms in preventing the spread of AIDS can help to develop students' understanding. These issues demonstrate the complex relationship between the public under-

---

ACTIVITIES

Find a copy of your school's SRE policy. Make sure you know what is taught in the PSHE programme and what the accepted school position is in relation to the key issues.

Think about the ground rules that you would expect to put in place in a science lesson where students might be talking about sex and relationships, and how you might respond if you were asked a question that could be embarrassing for you or a student.

standing of science and other influences on people's decisions and lifestyles.

Climate change

The evidence around climate change strongly supports the idea that human activity, and specifically the carbon emissions from burning fossil fuels, is leading to a global warming effect, with serious environmental consequences. However, there are various opposing views.

The question for you is how you position this debate in teaching the science. There is great value in the principle of presenting evidence and encouraging students to draw their own conclusions. However, here, the crucial point is that the evidence for man-made climate change is overwhelming relative to the scale of evidence to the contrary.

It would be wrong to present the case as '50:50 – *you decide*'. The most important thing to do is to make sure your students know enough of the science so that they can participate in discussions about global warming on an informed basis. Too often, students are asked to take a view, without really having enough knowledge with which to make a sound judgement.

Animal rights

You may encounter this topic as a general issue in society or, more directly, when you are performing dissections of animals, or even just their organs. This is not controversial: students have every right to express objections on the basis of their personal view regarding animal welfare. If a student expresses concerns, take them seriously and try to make arrangements that are mutually acceptable.

Nuclear power

The debate around the safety and overall value of nuclear power runs continually, fuelled in recent years by the Fukushima incident in Japan. Here, there is plenty of science to teach: the functions of a nuclear reactor; the nature of radiation and radioactive waste; the energy output relative to other sources; the impact of radiation on living tissues; the relative costs of commissioning and decommissioning power plants; and the scope to make them 'clean'.

For a science teacher, this topic is one where a fairly open debate is warranted. However, you need to guide students towards understanding the real benefits and dangers, steering them away from tabloid tales of mutant fish and babies with two heads ... the doomsday scenario.

Your role is not to tell students what to think; it is to show them how to work out what to think, based on evidence.

TALKING POINTS

1 How far do you go in questioning what we know or think we know about nature? Is it acceptable to just present science as a factual truth, at least most of the time?

2 Where do you draw the line in imposing your personal ethical and moral standpoint or your personal view of science and religion?

3 How does the development of scientific concepts over the course of history mirror a ladder of incremental conceptual understanding that can be used for teaching? How would you mitigate the risk of confusing students by telling them about incorrect theories from the past?

3 The science curriculum

Normally, when you start teaching in a new school, you will have three key sources of information to help with your planning:

1 an official statement of the curriculum: either the National Curriculum documents, which tend to give broad statements, or the exam board specifications, which are usually very detailed;

2 the school's in-house scheme of work or, increasingly, 'scheme of learning'; this will make more specific references to the resources in the school and will represent the thinking of your colleagues and their predecessors;

3 the textbooks in the department, which may or may not be linked closely to the exam specification or the scheme of work.

You will also have an ocean of material on the Internet to browse through and countless resources in filing cabinets around your department.

However, the key message of this chapter is that the science curriculum isn't something you merely follow; it is something you create. The curriculum that students experience depends to a massive degree on how ideas are constructed by the teacher. Even if you are working to the requirements of an examination or following the National Curriculum, you have enormous scope and significant autonomy to design your own, to shape what students will learn and how they'll learn it.

At first, it can be daunting, contemplating the scale of the science curriculum, and it is perfectly sensible to start out working from the existing books and documents to get you going. However, as soon as you can, you should try to take ownership of it for yourself. Actually, you can't really avoid it, but, in the end, this is the element of teaching that ultimately will sustain you throughout your career.

Every time you teach a topic – or even the same lesson, to different students – it changes. You find different ways to express the ideas, you make new connections between ideas and you develop a better understanding of how different students piece together the giant puzzle of scientific understanding.

More importantly, it's a hallmark of any great science teacher that they take ownership of the curriculum. They blend expert subject knowledge with expert pedagogy to create a curriculum experience for their students that is simultaneously rigorous, engaging and enlightening, going far beyond the confines of the textbook or the requirements of the exam. This is the ultimate goal.

The big picture

I find it extremely helpful to remind myself of the big picture, before looking at the detail.

Unlike subjects such as history and English, where there is a great deal of debate around what should be taught, science is relatively uncontroversial – though not completely. Science is fairly well defined as a subject.

Take a look at the contents page of any KS3 science textbook and you will find that they all have virtually identical content. This is partly because they are written to cover the content of the National Curriculum. At GCSE and A level, there is more divergence, but there is still a great deal of overlap between all the major examination board specifications.

If you try to break down the three main sciences into ten key topics, you might come up with something like my table here. This is the whole of science at a glance!

	Physics	Biology	Chemistry
1	Energy	Cells and organs	States of matter
2	Heat	Body systems	Elements and compounds
3	Forces	Digestion and nutrition	Chemical reactions
4	Motion	Gas exchange and respiration	Bonding
5	Space	Microbes and disease	Acids and bases
6	Waves	Photosynthesis and plant growth	Reactivity and periodic table
7	Electromagnetic spectrum	Ecosystems	Metals
8	Electricity	Carbon and nitrogen cycles	Hydrocarbons
9	Electromagnetism	Reproduction and genetics	Earth science
10	Constituents of matter	Evolution	Rates of reaction

It is worth spending some time reflecting on this table. Although not completely exhaustive, it is an attempt to capture the essence of our curriculum in one place. Straight away you notice a number of things:

Firstly, many of the topics overlap. Energy can be a pure physics topic, but is clearly an essential idea in explaining chemical reactions and many biological processes. The three sciences are interconnected. It makes sense to build each area of knowledge on a foundation of key concepts students have learned before, which has implications for your planning of the topic sequence. It also means you need to communicate with other teachers in your department, especially where you share a class with different specialist colleagues.

Secondly, there is a continuum within each science, for example between cells, organs and body systems; the topic divisions are somewhat arbitrary. Topics are rarely discrete and self-contained; the ideas contained within them could be turned into a massive, sprawling, interconnected mind map or spider diagram. Here, the challenge is to make a potentially complex set of ideas appear straightforward, while not simplifying too much so that real meaning is lost.

Again, there is a need for careful sequencing. Both of these points suggest a need for *coherence* in our curriculum. Although we have freedom to explore and experiment, ideas need to hang together in a sensible order. The design of any learning episode should reference what has gone before and what is likely to follow.

Thirdly, if you ask yourself what you understand about each topic, the answers will vary in depth. It is possible to know and understand each of these topics at different levels. It is often possible to give a Year 2 answer, a Year 9 answer or an A level answer to the same question. So, we need to consider how we're going to return to these topics and ideas over time, so that we can build up students' understanding at an appropriate time, without it feeling excessively repetitive. This is where the concept of '*spiralling*' comes in, alongside the important matter of *differentiation* covered in the next chapter.

Finally, how you teach each of these topics will shape how the students experience them. A series of lessons on the rock cycle as part of earth science could become very dry and book-bound. Students can learn in abstract terms what igneous or sedimentary rock looks like, along with a host of other related facts, without developing a strong conceptual understanding of geological timescales or the scale of the forces involved in tectonic processes.

However, if you also take them to stand under a cliff where the story of Earth's epochs and crust dynamics is laid bare – or use media resources that bring that experience into the classroom – then the learning will be different. Here, the question is more about 'how' than 'what'.

Similarly, sitting in a classroom, talking about rainforests and plant life can seem irrelevant. It's generally true that students are a lot less excited by plants than teachers, who might see gardening as a hobby. So, rather than talking about plants in general, it helps to talk about 'this plant here'. In other words, use real plants that they can see with their own eyes and take some interest in.

Of course, over and above the question of which resources you select, the factor in determining how well students learn and how much interest they take will be the quality of your explanations and the extent to which you succeed in communicating the idea that rocks and plants are fascinating and worth knowing more about.

Looking at the table, there will be areas where you'll have ideas bubbling away – too many to use. Here, you need to select. You won't have time to include every idea you ever have. There will be others where you may be struggling to know exactly what strategy would work. Try one.

ACTIVITIES

Identify your weaker areas. Where are you less sure of your own knowledge and pedagogical repertoire? That's where you should actively look to expand and develop. Find the relevant textbooks that cover these areas, with supporting exam questions and mark schemes, and study them. Prioritise those areas that you will be teaching in the near future.

The 'enacted curriculum'

Look at these examples:

CRUMPLE ZONES

Year 10 students are learning about momentum and the significance of this concept in car design. From a theoretical perspective, students have learned that change in momentum = average force × time for the collision. They are exploring the impact on a truck carrying an egg when rolled down a ramp into a barrier. By creating a cardboard crumple zone on the truck, they are testing whether they can maximise the collision time, thereby reducing the force and keeping the egg intact.

REACTION RATE

Year 11 students are learning about variables that determine the rate of a reaction but exploring the reaction between hydrochloric acid and sodium thiosulphate. When mixed, the reaction yields a suspension of sulphur that makes the solution increasingly cloudy. If placed in a flask over a cross on paper, the time for the cross to disappear gives a measure for the rate.

This is a standard experiment, but, in this case, the challenge set to the students is to adjust the concentrations of the solutions so that the cross disappears in exactly 23 seconds. They need to decide which variables to control in order to adjust the reactants until they get the required outcome.

FAMILY TREE

I have a printed scroll showing a single ancestral line from my children all the way back to William the Conqueror – my son's thirtieth great-grandfather. This artefact leads nicely to the consideration of the notion of 'common ancestors' in general, which features in the topic on heredity and evolution. If you do the maths (2^{30}, assuming two offspring per generation, on average), it is likely that most Caucasian English people are also descendants of William the Conqueror! My children and I may be 'royalty', but then we all are.

Working our way back in time, we reach a point between 10,000 and 100,000 years ago when a single person lived, from whom every living person on Earth is descended. As recently as that! It turns out that we are literally all cousins . . . a beautiful thought to share with your class. Using real family histories can help to contextualise the more theoretical elements of genetics and evolution.

This is the 'enacted curriculum' in action. Although you can link each example to a standard GCSE syllabus, you won't be told to use these examples in exactly this way. It's up to you. The curriculum enacted in your lessons will never be the same as the curriculum your colleague is enacting in the lab next door. This is both a great freedom and a great responsibility. But don't worry: help is always at hand!

The key is to build up a core framework of concepts that you can embellish and develop over time, in parallel with a set of learning activities that support it. The way you teach and what you teach are linked; they are mutually reinforcing strands of planning a great science curriculum. Even if you have a strong academic background, you will learn more about science the more you teach, and this, coupled with your developing science pedagogy, will provide material for future classes.

Creating your 'enacted curriculum'

In order to plan what to teach, it is helpful to consider three aspects of the topic in your planning:

Firstly, what do I *have* to teach?

Coverage of the syllabus for an exam or even an internal test is non-negotiable. You need to make sure that you plan the curriculum so that everything that will be assessed in any exam is included. This requires getting to grips with the specifications or looking ahead to see what the topic tests are like.

It might be tempting to see 'Cells' as a topic heading and then dive in, teaching what you want to about cells. However, there will be all kinds of nuance and emphasis that you need to pick up on in the syllabus, like it or not. The way questions are asked in past papers will tell you a lot about how an exam board sees the subject.

'Teaching to the test' is usually rightly criticised as an approach, because it leaves out so much of what science is about and is not compatible with learning in its broadest sense. However, in order to do justice to your students, you must ensure that the material in a test or exam is a subset of what you cover in your curriculum.

Secondly, what do I *want* to teach?

Beyond the confines of the syllabus, there is plenty of scope to bring in your own ideas. You will develop your own repertoire of favourite experiments and demonstrations soon enough. You will also have areas of specialist knowledge that you just enjoy sharing. Textbooks and the departmental scheme of work are meant to be there to help you – not to confine you. You may inherit a situation where there is a tight prescriptive regime, driven by the timetable or the equipment requisition system. However, even in very tight scenarios, you'll find you still have a lot of decisions to make about the 'what' and the 'how' of any given topic. So, don't hold back ... bring it all in.

Thirdly, *how* am I going to teach it?

This is the tough part, especially early on. There are so many options in most areas, and so this is mainly a case of filtering and selecting, running with some specific plans. You should then evaluate how successful you have been and be prepared to try other approaches another time.

Of course, these questions might perhaps be better expressed together as, 'what are my students going to learn?'. Teaching and learning are obviously interrelated, but they are also fundamentally different. Our job isn't merely to pump out information, regardless of whether students are engaging with it and processing it. Hopefully, it is also true that our job isn't only to help them pass exams.

So, in planning your curriculum, it's often more powerful to think in terms of learning, rather than teaching. Now the questions become: What do they *have* to learn? What do I *want* them to learn? *How* are they going to learn? This set of questions also then introduces a fourth: What do *the students want to learn*?

Obviously, students can't decide what to learn if they don't know exactly what there is to learn. *However,* very often students do have a scientific interest that they want to pursue; they might be curious about something; they might have a question they've always wondered about. If so, it pays to give them some space to shape their own learning as part of the process.

Your Year 8 students might ask questions such as these:

- How come whales and hippos are so closely related?
- How do black holes form?
- Why am I colour blind like my granddad?
- How does HIV turn into AIDS?
- What is a bucky-ball?

What do you say? 'Wait until Year 10'? That's not going to cut it. Look at where you can give them scope to have input to the planned topic sequence where their questions can be dealt with, sooner rather than later. At the very least, you can ask them to go and find out and report back to the class – but you still need to give space for this to happen.

Core concepts

Some ideas in science are so central that everything else hinges on them. I'd include particles, energy, rate of change, chemical and physical change, conservation laws, experimental methodology, units of measurement and scale. As a science teacher, it is really important to understand these ideas well yourself, as you will come back to them repeatedly.

Particles

Across the entirety of a school life, students will develop an ever more sophisticated idea about the structure of matter and how materials are made up of particles – either as atoms, molecules or ions. It is very important to use these terms correctly and to challenge students if they mix them up at a point when they should know the difference. This is where coherence kicks in. You can't teach about chemical reactions or vapourisation until students have a reasonable concept of materials being made up of atoms or molecules.

If we're introducing particles, we might look at sugar or salt: two white, granulated substances. It's possible to imagine dividing them up into ever finer pieces, until we start to imagine 'building blocks' that can't be subdivided further. The aim is to develop a mental model for the idea that all substances are macroscopic manifestations of billions of relatively simple particles, joined together.

At the beginning of this particular learning path, there is no point getting bogged down in distinguishing between salt as an ionically bonded, giant lattice structure and sugar as a molecular compound. This is too much detail. Similarly, it is sensible to stop at 'atoms', without needing to delve further to discuss electrons, hadrons and quarks.

Once students can talk about particles, it is easier to discuss a wide range of phenomena:

- the difference between ice, water and steam, despite their being made of identical molecules;

- digestion as the breaking down of large molecules into smaller ones that can fit through holes in the tissues that line the digestive system organs;

- evaporation as a process by which the most energetic molecules continually escape the surface of a liquid . . . until it has all vapourised;

- the thermal decomposition of green copper carbonate to form black copper oxide with the release of carbon dioxide;

- diffusion of smells across a room as the random movement of gas particles interacting with air molecules via a series of collisions;

- the idea that a person standing on a table, on a macro scale, is actually being held up by attractive forces between molecules of wood, balancing the force of gravity.

Without a strong model for particles, these phenomena, at their everyday macro-scale, are virtually impossible to comprehend. 'The puddle just disappears!', 'The green stuff turns into black stuff!', 'Ice reacts with heat to make water', and so on.

ACTIVITY

Explore your understanding of these phenomena. How would you use a particle model, illustrated with diagrams, to explain them to a class?

The science curriculum

It is important to pitch the learning at the right level, so that you are not locking in incorrect ideas. I find that even very sophisticated students can lapse into using molecule, ion and atom almost interchangeably, as if they don't really matter, long after it really does! This then inhibits their understanding: hydrogen gas reacts with oxygen as it does because it is a molecule, H_2. In its ionic form, H^+, it behaves differently.

So, your job is to map this out. At each new level of depth, you need to give students the time to reconfigure their mental models. It helps to refer to diagrams and visual models to develop a deeper understanding of atoms and molecules. For a teacher, a good understanding of the kinetic theory of particles is really important, as it is something you return to over and over again.

However, take care with diagrams. An example often cited by Dylan Wiliam is of a teacher who showed her class a diagram of water molecules: lots of H=O=H molecules arranged on a page. Students could reproduce this diagram on request to show what

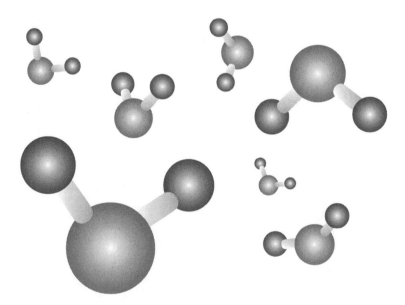

Figure 3.1 Molecules of water

water looked like. Did this show they understood the molecular nature of water? No. Why? Because, when asked, 'where is the water?', several students pointed to the space in between the molecules; they'd failed to grasp that the molecules *were* the water.

Energy

Energy is a term that has a good foundation in everyday language, usually used in a scientifically plausible context. People will talk about needing to eat to 'get some energy inside them'; they'll listen to a news story about the 'energy crisis' when the price of gas and electricity is being discussed; they will describe someone who runs around doing a lot as being energetic and will be comfortable with the idea that some tasks need more energy than others to complete. Food packaging has energy content on the labels, and younger students can readily relate to the idea that some foods provide more energy than others.

However, when we start to formalise things, energy can become rather abstract. Although it is a quantity that can be measured in certain units, it is still intangible. You can't hold it in your hands. Similarly, the idea that energy can take various forms without any of it getting lost or destroyed is a big leap.

In Chapter 7, an energy circus is one of the examples of a classic circus-style class practical. In some ways, the whole of science is a study of energy transfers, and so you are going to be talking about it in almost every context:

- food webs and food chains and the pyramid of biomass;
- storing energy from food, for example after photosynthesis in plants, and then releasing it through respiration;
- heat released and absorbed in chemical reactions of various kinds;
- the idea that most reactions naturally progress in one direction only, because of the need to break and form bonds; the idea of 'activation energy';

- the concepts of kinetic and potential energy, escaping Earth's gravitational field or simply lifting your own body up some stairs;

- the capacity of electrical energy to transfer to many forms – making motors, lights, heaters, loud speakers, and so on;

- waves as a means of transferring energy.

Considering how often we talk about energy, it is surprising how late we tend to teach the concept of 'work done', using force multiplied by distance, and the related definition of the unit of a joule. However, in your spiralling curriculum, you need to know roughly when this happens. Students can live with a general idea that energy is measured in joules, without knowing what a joule is, so don't overburden them too early.

However, once you can start linking a joule to 'a Newton moving 1 m', the size of a joule begins to make sense, and lots more ideas can start to interlink. It is useful to have some ready reckoners at hand. For example, if you lift a 1 kg bag of sugar by 10 cm, you have used 1 joule of energy. So a kilojoule is the energy needed to

ACTIVITY

Explore your understanding of energy transfers in terms of forms of energy, scale and units. What is the energy scale involved in food webs, nuclear power or a petrol engine? Examine the idea of 'energy loss' – given that energy must be conserved – and the mechanism for energy being dissipated into the environment as heat that is too diluted to capture or put to use. My favourite example is banging a table with my hand: after the event, energy has been transferred as sound, but eventually it has all been dissipated via molecules in my hand, the table and the air all having slightly higher than average kinetic energy.

lift 1 tonne (1,000 kg) by 10 cm – or to lift that bag of sugar by 100 m, or by 10 cm a thousand times.

If you compare that with a chocolate bar – a typical value of say 350 kJ per 100 g – you can start to put the numerical values of energy into context and make it all seem less abstract. A 100 W bulb gives out 100 J of energy every second; a 2 kW kettle uses 2,000 J of energy per second, and so on. You build up the picture over time, linking back to energy as each topic comes along.

Scale

Scale as a concept is rarely taught as a discrete topic, but it permeates all topics to some degree. As part of forming mental models that, in turn, help students to explain key phenomena, working out the scale is important. Here, this isn't about precision; it is about a rough order of magnitude. Often, relative scale is expressed through analogies with macro-scale objects, but we also need to try to see scale directly, if at all possible.

In biology, scale is nicely dealt with by using microscopes. A typical blood cell, cheek cell or onion cell can be seen with a low-power school microscope. Through microscope work, students start to realise that there are other worlds beneath the macro world they operate in.

Another example of this is the study of grass as an ecosystem. If you ask students to lie down on grass and peer into a localised area, it takes on a totally different scale. All kinds of insects and plant varieties become apparent. You can also extract a lot of learning from catching insects in a 'pooter' trap and examining them with a simple magnifying glass. A concept of scale develops simply from changing the students' perspective and asking them to look up close at things they see every day.

Getting the sense of the size of an atom is interesting, but a lot more difficult. There are lots of websites, photographs and pieces of software that provide models of this. But how can you do it in a classroom? Try this:

The science curriculum

Firstly, ask students to look at the lines on a ruler, mentally dividing each millimetre into ten smaller divisions. They can just see this. They then have to visualise mini cubes that are 0.1 × 0.1 × 0.1 mm in size. Now, imagine a line of cubes along a 1 m rule. There will be 10,000 of them.

If we scale up the model further to a 100 m running track, there will be 1 million cubes in a line. Dwell on this for a while to get students to visualise this line. Finally, imagine that the whole line of 1 million cubes is shrunk down to fit along the edge of just one of the 0.1 mm cubes. We now have 1 million cubes sitting along a 0.1 mm line. That's about the size of an atom. It is head-spinning, and, for most purposes, you can gloss over this. However, it pays to invest in this kind of model-building repeatedly.

The size of a nucleus relative to an atom is another classic scale model. A common example is to say it is like a pea at the centre of a football pitch, with the electrons whizzing around the stands. The key learning here is that most of an atom is empty space! For many students, all this is very abstract, and they will barely grasp it. However, there will be students who can deal with this complexity and will want to grapple with it. Try linking this atomic model to the cubes-on-the-ruler model . . . the stadium needs to shrink down to fit into one of the shrunken mini cubes!

Another important idea is the number of atoms in a mole of a substance. This helps get a sense of atomic size, but also puts chemical and biological processes into perspective. The number of atoms in 12 g of carbon – 12 is 6.02×10^{23} – Avogadro's number. How big is this? One way to visualise it is to compare it with grains of sand on a beach: there are more atoms in a grain of sand, than grains of sand on a beach. Or, the one I like is to reference it to time. The universe is about 10 billion years old, and, in each year, there are over 30 milllion seconds. So, if we were to count the atoms in a pin head, one atom each second, it would take longer than the age of the universe.

A similar scaling process is useful to capture the size of our solar system, or the distance to the nearest star after our Sun. Moving up from Earth–Moon, to Earth–Sun, to solar system, galaxy and distance to the next nearest galaxy are all big questions that require a mental model of sorts. Describing the large scale of our universe is important to understanding the limitations on space travel and to developing a proper understanding of just how remote Earth is.

In science generally, knowing the size of any quantity is useful. From life experience, we know the size of 1 m and the length of 1 minute relative to other lengths and times, but most other units need to be given a context. Whenever you introduce a new quantity with new units, it is useful to put it in perspective. Teslas and couloumbs are huge units for magnetic field strength and charge, respectively. A 100 A current would be enormous (domestic fuses are 13 A); 100 m/s is ten times faster than Usain Bolt; 100 Pa is a very low pressure – atmospheric pressure is 100 kPa, the equivalent of carrying several hundred kilograms on our heads all day!

Scale in perspective

Although I've just outlined some ideas for exploring the true scale of numbers of particles and their size, we mustn't lose sight of the fact that we all experience science on a real-life macro-scale. As discussed in Chapter 2, models are only approximations, and we are asking students to make a very significant leap in relating our simplified diagrams to the macro phenomena they observe with their own eyes.

The trick is to continually make references back and forth from the models to the macro. The stylised, idealised plant 'form and function' diagram, showing all the cellular structures in the roots, stem and leaves, is an essential piece of learning. The photographs of microscope slides showing specimens of root hairs or stomata guard cells are fascinating. But you also need to set them alongside some real plants, so that students can make the connections in terms of their own sense of scale.

Spiralling the curriculum

In seeking to plan your curriculum or to make sense of a prescribed scheme of work, you need to know how the elements spiral over time. This means that you need to find out what ideas students have already encountered and at what level. Similarly, you need some idea of where the ideas will be encountered later on. This will help you gauge the pitch of individual lessons and determine how much to worry if any number of students doesn't fully grasp an idea.

It is supremely important not to teach a topic assuming that students know nothing about it. There is a big difference between taking an idea further forward and simply repeating what was done before. This issue is acute in Year 7, when students arrive from primary school. Before you launch into 'doing the basics', find out what they can already do. You'll be amazed: amazed at how different their experiences have been and how far some have gone.

However, the same principle applies every time you take on a new class or meet a new student. You can teach the same topics, but the question is where to pitch the content for the individuals in the class.

See the table (facing page) for spiralling in action.

The table illustrates how the same concepts can be explained at different levels. There are certainly intermediary levels between those shown and levels beyond. A good spiral curriculum will allow you to return to the key topics at suitable intervals, so that the ideas can be taken further. The goal is to teach them the first time so that students are engaged and develop a solid core of understanding, sowing the seeds of what will come later; the aim in subsequent spirals is to move forward, so that it feels fresh, picking up where students left off, not just where you want to start.

Pulling all this together, there will be a number of factors to consider that relate to your specific circumstances: the ability profile of the class, the time available for the overall course and the resources at your disposal. In the next chapter, we'll look at the thorny issue of differentiation and the implications for planning.

Topic	Basic level	Advanced level
Respiration	We need energy from our food to do exercise; to run we need to pump food around our bodies faster, so our muscles get the energy they need; we also need to breathe in more, because oxygen in air is needed to release energy from food; food and oxygen travel in our blood, so our heart has to beat faster, and we breathe faster during exercise	The equation for respiration is: $$\text{Glucose} + O_2 \rightarrow CO_2 + H_2O + \text{energy}$$ Gaseous exchange in the lungs and rate of blood flow increase to deliver O_2 and expel CO_2. Hence heart rate and breathing rate increase during exercise Insufficient O_2 leads to anaerobic respiration, resulting in lactic acid build-up, which can be experienced as cramp
Ecosystems	Food chains exist in local environments. Some animals only eat plants; others eat smaller animals. Predators eat their prey. There are usually fewer larger predators at the top of the food chain. Sudden changes in the environment can upset the balance of numbers of each animal	Food webs are part of an ecosystem where habitat, predation and disease all play a role. Population sizes vary over time, depending on a range of factors; sudden environmental change or new predators can result in extinctions. Energy transferred as biomass forms a pyramid up the food chain from producers to consumers
Light	Rays of light travel in straight lines; they reflect from shiny surfaces so that the angles are equal; they bend where materials meet – as with glass. This helps to make lenses and explains why a stick looks bent in water	Light is made up of photons of varying wavelengths and frequencies. Different materials slow light down by varying degrees; refraction occurs at the boundary between media of different refractive index. The angles follow the equation $n = \sin i / \sin r$

TALKING POINTS

1   In what way will the 'enacted curriculum' in your lessons differ from the prescribed curriculum written down in the scheme of work?

2   For the key concepts in your schemes of work for the coming year, how are you going to ensure that the spiralling is achieved successfully?

3   How do you tackle the spiralling issue when the starting point of different students will vary, often from topic to topic?

4 Planning for differentiation

You might imagine that teaching science is such a well-travelled journey that schools would have got the whole process of what works and what doesn't mapped out by now.

However, as we explored in the last chapter, the essence of teaching is making the curriculum come to life in your classroom, with your specific students. In that sense, as you are creating the curriculum, each lesson is unique. It isn't uncharted water – there are lots of standard reference points – but it is down to you to navigate the course. This is about planning.

More specifically, it means planning for the individual students travelling with you. This is about differentiation. They are inextricably linked.

For most teachers, in most schools, planning will take three forms: long-term, medium-term and short-term plans.

The long-term plan

This is the big picture. It might set out an overview of a whole year's work, or even the whole of a GCSE or A level course. In my current department, we have an A4 GCSE overview and a document called 'The timeline'. This is the key reference point for checking on our progress through the A level course.

Planning for differentiation

Your long-term plan is important, because it will give you a sense of how to pace your lessons across several weeks and months. Without a long-term plan, you can find that you've drifted quite a long way, getting bogged down in one topic area. The price you then pay is being forced to rush through other topics later on, in order to get back on track.

Often, the reason for losing time is a sense that students need more time to fully get to grips with a topic before you can move on. This is a feeling that almost never goes away. You rarely feel that everyone has absolutely nailed a concept, with all the misconceptions and areas of confusion squared away. However, it is important to balance depth of learning in each specific area with secure coverage of the whole curriculum. It's always a compromise.

I find it useful to think about learning as a series of arcs. At the start of a learning sequence, you throw up various ideas and concepts. There is some confusion and uncertainty. Then, you engage in various activities that start to put these ideas into some order, making sense of the confusion. Finally, the learning comes down to land. Some arcs can be completed within a lesson; others take weeks – or months – and, crucially, the landing moment will be different for each student.

So, you need to develop a tolerance for a degree of confusion and convey confidence to your students that this is a normal part of the learning process. To learn is to struggle . . . at least for a while. The landing moment will come, but sometimes it takes the time it takes.

After you've moved on for while, you can return to consolidate ideas as you spiral around again, or engage in revision activities. Of course, there will be times when some students will need additional support, and knowing when to give that is one of the subtler skills you'll develop over time.

The medium-term plan

This is usually the same thing as the scheme of work for a topic. I've seen examples that are incredibly elaborate, detailing every lesson in a series, giving specific questions, listing particular practical activities, indicating the homework that could be set and suggesting a range of alternatives for providing extra support and extra challenge.

In one school I worked at, it was possible to order 'Electricity lesson 3b' or 'Metals lesson 6d' from the technicians, and that would result in some specific equipment being delivered to the classroom. This was useful in some respects, but I soon found it limiting, and it meant I didn't put enough of my own ideas into the planning process. I was essentially delivering someone else's lessons, not my own.

This 'kitchen sink' approach to planning certainly removes the need to think too much about what to do, week on week, which can provide a sense of security. It can also help to share out the workload across a team. However, it can also feel rigid. You might prefer plans that are more skeletal, giving you a broad outline of the types of activity that could be covered, but leaving the detail more open. You will have your own preference, although, to begin with, it's likely you'll be working from your school's template.

It's at the level of the medium term that I do most of my planning. On this scale, you can map out the range of learning activities you want your students to experience, while still giving yourself scope to be spontaneous and responsive.

I think of this as 'contingent planning'. You are setting out a set of possibilities, but allowing the learning flow to dictate exactly which direction you take and how quickly you move from one thing to the next. I don't usually think more than one or two lessons ahead, although I have an idea of where we are going and routinely set out timeline markers that we need to reach.

A typical medium-term plan is likely to include a range of different learning modes:

- some whole-class teaching, with teacher demonstrations and stimulus material, followed by extensive opportunities to answer questions that cement the learning;

Planning for differentiation

- class practicals, where students follow a fairly standard procedure to make observations or take measurements;

- an extended investigation, where students design their own procedures to test out a hypothesis;

- opportunities to engage in problem-solving, either individually or in collaboration with others, using both mathematics and extended writing;

- some research tasks that involve presenting information in a number of forms, or taking the lead in teaching a group or the whole class;

- an element of choice or a creative task that gives students opportunities to make decisions and to explore ideas on their own terms;

- perhaps some formalised discussion or debate around some of the ethical, social or environmental issues in science;

- formative assessment tasks that help students give and receive feedback about the level of their understanding.

These are explored in more detail in Chapters 6 and 7.

If you can build in diversity in a planned way, then you are going to have a good chance of engaging your students and ensuring that learning in a range of forms is going to take place. In my opinion, the medium term is the level at which you should try to build in variety, not within individual lessons. Over time, students will value science more as a subject if they experience its multidisciplinary quality.

In the age of hyper-accountability, my advice is to do all you can so that you don't get sucked into thinking you need to pack all this into one lesson, making a giant song and dance to impress an external observer. The analogy I use is of the balanced diet. Over a month, you might enjoy a range of gourmet meals, some functional but tasty feed-ups, some routine staples and some special treats – the things you really love to eat. To eat healthily, you'll make sure you have a balanced diet overall. But imagine compressing all that delicious food into a kind of nutritional paste that you eat day after day. The nutrients might be the same in theory, but the essence of food as a pleasurable experience with intrinsic value is lost.

The analogy is clear. Teaching effectively is not about grinding out formulaic lessons day after day, nor delivering hyperactive, overloaded showcases. It's about delivering a wide range of simple and effective lessons that provide variety over time. And, of course, from time to time, you'll dazzle.

The short-term plan

This is the plan for a specific lesson or, at most, the lessons for a particular week. As before, there are lots of ways to do it, some more detailed than others. At first, you will want to write some lesson plans in detail, but, increasingly, you'll find that you just need to sketch out a rough outline. However, there are some common requirements, whether explicitly stated or just stored in your head, as you think through the lessons for the week.

A lesson plan should include:

* explicit links to the learning that has gone before;
* a set of learning aims for that lesson;
* the core planned activities;
* the resources and equipment that you need;
* the key mode of feedback;
* the homework.

Let's go through those in more detail:

Explicit links to the learning that has gone before and that will follow: If you are starting something new, you must plan activities that tease our prior learning. It also helps students to know how any one lesson fits into the wider context.

Planning for differentiation

A set of learning aims for that lesson: It could be just one simple aim, or learning objective, or it could be several. However, everything you do in the lesson needs to be driven by the question: What do I want students to learn in this lesson? In other words, you need to focus on what the learning points are, rather than merely thinking about the tasks that students will do. As we'll see later, this is critical when we are planning practical work. You need to be really clear about what it's for. It is also an important aspect of formative assessment.

So, instead of thinking 'we're doing a lesson on cells', you need to be thinking 'I want students to be able to identify the key similarities and differences between plant and animal cells'. Instead of thinking in general terms about 'the properties of metals', you should think about a more precise learning outcome: 'I want students to know that metals react with acids to release hydrogen gas and they conduct heat and electricity because of the presence of free electrons'. If you are 'doing electrolysis', you should be thinking about a learning outcome such as 'knowing that the positive ions will be attracted to the negative electrode, called the cathode, where they gain electrons'.

The core planned activities: You need to ask: What am I going to do? What are the students going to do, and in what configuration of groupings? How will these activities help to secure the learning? You might also have a rough idea of the timing for the lesson, to allow you to get through everything. When teachers feel their lesson didn't go as well as they'd have liked, mistiming is commonly the issue. Very often, this is a result of planning a 'snappy starter activity' that simply dragged on too long.

It is worth spelling out at this point that you do not need to plan starter activities. They can be engaging; they can be effective behaviour management devices; they can lead to real thinking and learning. However, if you've got a lot to get on with, and time will be tight or unpredictable, ditch the starter. Just get straight on.

The resources and equipment that you need: This may seem obvious enough, but the point to remember is the role good resources play. Excellent resources – either on paper, via multi-media, in books or in the form of various bits of apparatus – can make a lesson work superbly, if they support the key learning aims. However, I have seen teachers prepare great resources without paying enough attention to how they would be used. Students end up 'doing a worksheet', watching a video or using some software, but not actually making progress towards any specific learning aim. Invariably, these lessons feel low quality and lacking in challenge. By the same token, shoddy resources can ruin a lesson. It cuts both ways. Ideally, we want high-quality resources, tightly linked to learning aims.

In Chapter 7, we will revisit the issue of planning practical work extensively. Science is a practical subject, and planning the equipment you need, working with your technician team, is going to play a major role in your life as a science teacher.

The key mode of feedback: You need to give thought to how you will structure your questioning, how you will give feedback from the previous lesson or piece of work and whether you need any special resources – the success criteria, a set of mini-whiteboards, and so on.

The homework: the work you will set students to do between lessons. This may well depend on how the lesson progresses, but it is useful to have options planned in advance. I'm a firm believer in the power of homework as a vehicle for setting standards, providing learning opportunities that extend learning beyond the confines of a classroom, and for giving students scope to consolidate learning at their own pace.

Generally speaking, it pays off to be one of the teachers who is regarded as strong in terms of homework setting, and you will reap the rewards later on.

Firstly, students need to learn how to organise their learning in between lessons, especially when it comes to revising for exams. Routine homework can help them to do this, because it requires them to develop habits and routines based around independent study.

Planning for differentiation

Secondly, parents can engage with their children's school work by seeing the homework they get; a teacher setting some interesting and challenging homework will go up in their estimation, and that can lead them to being more supportive and encouraging.

Thirdly, different students will benefit from different forms of homework. A top-end student will often thrive on the opportunity to do some extended, open-ended, challenging work. They'll relish the chance to shine and show what they can do. However, students who struggle and don't have people at home who can help when they get stuck can find homework knocks their confidence. Showing an awareness of this in your homework setting is part of the planning process.

It follows that it is worth spending time planning good homework activities.

In the early stages of your teaching career, detailed planning like this helps you to think through how a lesson will work, and you reap the rewards. However, over time, many of these elements become organic, and, with a few bullet-pointed notes, the rest is implied. On top of that, you need to remain agile at all times. Lessons rarely go exactly according to plan. If the learning needs

---

ACTIVITIES

Take one unit of work that you are likely to teach in the near future. Sketch out a medium-term plan, thinking about how you might build in a variety of modes of teaching and learning across the whole unit.

Take one of the lessons and map out a plan that covers the points as set out above. What are the learning aims? How will you give feedback? What would make a good homework activity?

Discuss both of your plans with a more experienced colleague.

of the students or unforeseen circumstances dictate that a change of course is needed, the confidence to abandon a plan is as important as the plan itself.

Differentiation: one size does not fit all

So far, we've been talking about the students in the class as a group at roughly the same stage in their learning. However, the big challenge in all of this is that your students will all be different. You may teach in groups that are set by ability, you may have a mixed-ability group or you may teach in a selective school. Whatever the context, it's important to remember that every class is a mixed-ability class – even the narrowest of set groups.

You will need to cater for students with a range of skills, aptitudes and dispositions. One student's deep end is another's shallow end, and there is an important difference between a healthy period of struggling and drowning. The goal has got to be that all students make excellent progress, regardless of their starting point, without making things too safe, or beyond reach. Of course, the wider the ability range in a class, the more difficult and critical it is. It's a significant challenge, but not one that is insurmountable.

Reading this chapter, you may be thinking of a particular class that you teach, but let's imagine the range of students you might be dealing with in a typical secondary school class:

- Sabrina is supremely clever and conscientious. She will do everything you ask, neatly and quickly, and seems to grasp new ideas easily. She's a certain A* candidate.

- Jack never wants to write anything down but asks questions all the time. He is intuitive and enthusiastic and always puts his hand up, even if he doesn't really know the answer for sure. His book is a mess, but he manages to do comparatively well on tests.

- Daisy is a lively, engaging student, but she thinks she is rubbish at science. She is always checking to see what other people have done, lacking confidence in her own work. She is stressed by competitive answer calling and hangs back when questions are offered to the whole class; she will take a back seat during practical work, if given the choice.

- Michael is often disengaged. He defaults to chatting, swinging back on his chair and fidgeting. He takes a long time to draw a table or to get organised for writing, even if he has remembered his basic equipment.

- Harun speaks English as an additional language (EAL), but is very intelligent and is very good at maths. It is hard to separate his cognitive understanding from his confidence with English.

- Alicia is quiet. She joins in when encouraged, does most of the work, always performs averagely well when the class does a test and never causes trouble.

All the various learner characteristics will be found in limitless permutations and in varying numbers in any one class. Planning lessons where Sabrina, Jack, Daisy, Michael, Harun and Alicia all thrive is the daily challenge. How is it done?

Knowing the students

This is the bedrock of effective differentiation. The first steps to knowing your students should include learning their names. This may sound obvious, but it takes some effort. Setting out a seating plan is a good way to do this. It helps you to ask questions using names – by glancing quickly at your plan – and that has a powerful effect. You'll find that knowing names and dictating where students sit are also very powerful aspects of developing an assertive behaviour management style.

One of those often-unacknowledged classroom issues is that names are often very strongly linked to our ethnic or cultural heritage, where linguistic differences are strong. This means that you may have students whose names you find hard to remember or to pronounce. Talk to them about this and try hard to get it right. The sooner you know your students' names, the more confident you will feel, and the more supportive your students will be of you.

Over time, you will get to know your students as people, but it is knowing them as learners that is the most crucial. When you observe a highly skilled teacher deliver a great lesson, their nuanced knowledge of their students' needs is always evident. The best way to achieve this early on is to set some challenging work and to mark it yourself, so that you get a feel for a range of learning issues. You then have some information of your own to reference against the data record and the classroom interactions you observe.

In most schools, you will be presented with a range of data for the classes you teach. If it is not given to you, you must try to seek it out. The data might include the following:

- prior attainment measures: test scores from previous years or results in formal public exams;

- cognitive ability test scores derived from baseline tests at the start of Year 7; these might be referred to as CATs or MidYIS scores;

- the reading age of each student and the most recent information on any special education needs;

- information about their English language level and whether they speak EAL;

- target grade data suggesting the level of attainment students should reach if they follow or exceed the national trend, based on their prior attainment;

- you may also be given information about whether students are on a gifted and talented register, or whether they have free school meals or are entitled to the pupil premium.

Obviously enough, the data is largely irrelevant if it doesn't change your teacher–student interactions. You need to study the data to look for issues and to assimilate it into some useable knowledge. The data has to come off the page. Too great a volume of data can impede that process, so be wary of data-overload.

The goal is to engage with the data you have to a level that maximises the rate of progress of your students. You should use the information to fine-tune your planning and differentiation strategies; you should use it to give you the courage and confidence to set very challenging aspirations for each student. You must not allow data to suggest that you write students off or lead to you lowering your sights for them.

Using data

I've known teachers to glaze over at the sight of a busy spreadsheet, to the point where they barely engage with it at all. They may have the data pasted into their mark books, but it doesn't go any further. Obviously, you'll need to engage with each student on an individual level, but, at a planning level, to penetrate the rows of figures and codes, it pays dividends to highlight the key issues and to create some form of differentiation guide for each class that you teach.

The top end

Students with a clear record of high prior attainment need to be challenged; most, but not all, will expect it. You need to ensure that you hit the ground running with your most able students and then sustain that challenge level. The data can help to make explicitly clear who the key students are that will need this continual stretch and challenge, even when they may not show their potential directly. This is especially true of students who appear demotivated or lazy. Don't allow yourself to confuse motivation with ability – or, more importantly, low motivation with low ability.

The middle ground

These students are often the central battleground for raising attainment. If you can spot students who have made little progress in the last year, or who have very high scores in one area but not in another, make sure you get to know them very quickly. If you have data that indicates students with behaviour or motivational issues alongside strong prior attainment, then take note.

Students with low literacy levels

Students who are identified as having low reading ages or a low level of fluency in English need to be catered for so that they can access any written material. If you only ever give a child books they cannot read, they are not going to progress with their understanding of science as fast as the others. Act on this information by making sure you know the students concerned and by seeking out appropriate resources to help you.

Students with special educational needs

Students who are identified as SEN, covering a wide range of areas, will often have action plans and a raft of documentation about them on your school's systems. You really must not ignore this. Make sure you find out all you can and digest it. For example, if the SEN team feels that a student really needs to sit at the front of the class, for any number of reasons, then you should follow their recommendation. If you have counter-evidence later on, then, of course, you should feed that back. You should be given special advice about working with students with very specific disabilities – hearing or visually impaired students need strategies that are often unique to them – but make sure you seek this out and that you ask for help if you ever need it.

An important point to remember is that, when students are supported by the SEN department or even have a learning support assistant (LSA) allocated to help them in your lessons, they are still your responsibility. You must not assume that anyone else is taking control of their learning; it is your job to meet their needs, using the support provided. A common complaint of students who have a lot of time with an LSA is that their teacher doesn't directly talk to them enough.

Planning for differentiation

Taking all of this on board, perhaps the most important thing is to highlight the students who are likely to need significant additional support to thrive in your lessons, especially if you are going to be teaching to the top. These are students who you are most likely to have to prepare additional resources for on a routine basis.

ACTIVITY

When you are given a class to teach, get hold of the data that is available and undertake a thorough analysis. Reference this against your experience of teaching them, so that the data makes sense and come off the page, informing your future interactions with the individual students.

Adopt a 'growth mindset' instead of a 'fixed mindset'

Carol Dweck's work is now firmly associated with this concept (Dweck, 2006), but it has always been the case that, as teachers, we need to re-evaluate our view of our students continually. We can't ever assume a child is defined by the spreadsheet we were given at the start of term. So, beyond that first trawl through the data, try to engage with the tracking system in your school or department too. Some systems are quite elaborate. You must always keep the volume of data in perspective, doing your best to update your knowledge bank, which then guides you as you plan and deliver your lessons.

Of course, the most important source of information is the informal and formal feedback from your day-to-day interactions, alongside the information you glean from marking books and tests. You should also be open to feedback from parents. Very often, students will report to their parents that they are finding work too easy or too difficult, before you have noticed. Try never to be defensive or resistant to this kind of information; we need to listen and encourage dialogue with parents – to dismiss it is folly! Apart from anything, it helps to have parents on your side; a teacher who listens is someone parents trust and support. They'll love you for it.

Now what? You know your students, but what difference does it make? Assimilating all that information so that lesson activities and the level of challenge are finely tuned is the goal. Knowing your students is critical, but it is only the start. The point is that you do something with this knowledge.

'A total philosophy of gifted and talented provision'

Before getting into some of the specific strategies for differentiation, I want to suggest that, to be an effective teacher, you need to adopt a 'teach to the top' approach, catering explicitly for the needs of the most able students in your class as a priority. In my experience, it is the only way to fully meet the needs of every learner. If you pitch every lesson and the general thrust of every unit of work to stretch the most able, everyone benefits:

- The ablest students enjoy their learning, feel valued and feel normal.

- The parents of your ablest students give you lots of helpful support.

- The learning environment in each lesson is characterised by high expectations. This raises aspirations, and, through differentiation and support, all students are pulled along in the wake of the ablest.

In short, love-up your ablest students, and only good things will come; fall short in meeting their needs, and it can lead to under-achievement and justified frustration from parents.

What this means is that you don't pitch to the middle and then give the most able students a few extras; you only differentiate downwards, to support students to keep up with the ablest. At least, you try to do this to the greatest possible extent. This kind of approach will require you to do the following:

Ensure there is rigour and depth in the subject matter

Embrace the full complexity of a topic before breaking it down to make it accessible. Very able students love highly synoptic tasks, where they assimilate lots of layers of information and make sense of competing and contradictory points of view and messy data. They also want to know how and why things are as they are ... there is always another and another layer of 'but why ...?'. Allow this complexity to hang for a while before you bring it down and process it.

Model and celebrate the use of sophisticated language and terminology. For example, talk about mirrors in terms of light reflecting, not 'bouncing'; talk about molecules undergoing diffusion, not merely 'going through the cell wall'; use the language of increasing, decreasing and remaining constant, instead of 'going up, going down and staying the same'.

This is where it pays to really know your subject, so you can prepare those extra layers of questioning. Allow a good deal of 'struggle time' and don't give away the answers cheaply!

Create a classroom culture that celebrates intellectual curiosity

Maximise opportunities for students to engage in open-ended, problem-solving tasks and tasks that give students scope for a bit of creative eccentricity. Create a culture that turns all those pejoratives into badges of honour: geek, nerd, brainy. Champion students with a general, all-round passion for knowledge and understanding and never let anyone diminish them for it.

Set a demanding workload

It will pay dividends if you are one of the teachers who always set regular, challenging homework, have high expectations for the quality of classwork and are generally demanding. In doing this, you will be allowing students with an appetite for study to thrive; you will not be putting a lid on their expectations. Conversely, if you are ever soft in these areas, it can be undermining, and the ablest students will be the first to doubt you. Give them everything they need and no less. If the ablest students in a class start complaining of overload, then you know you're hitting the right level.

ACTIVITY

For a specific topic and year group, such as Year 9 genetics, think about the level the highest-performing students might be at. What content, terminology and concepts do you think you could bring in to stretch them fully? Test this out. Give them ever more challenging questions, until they find them genuinely difficult.

Differentiation strategies

Within the context of a 'teaching to the top' culture, in practice there are four main forms of differentiation that teachers typically deploy:

Different resources

- **Support material**: extra layers of scaffolding and simplification to help students keep up.
- **Extension material**: very typically, this is 'extra work' students can do if they've finished the standard work, but it can also be the built-in materials that only the most able students engage with.

Planning for differentiation

Some differentiated resources will be needed repeatedly and are worth preparing in advance and keeping handy in your classroom. These are typically pre-prepared materials for practical work:

- **Blank tables** with multiple columns for entering observations and measurements are very useful. In a mixed-ability class, you are likely to have a few students who find the mechanics of drawing a table very challenging. Obviously, this is a skill they need to practise. But, in the context of a busy lesson where the key learning is going to derive from the results, it is helpful to give them a ready-made table, instead of them wasting time struggling.

- **Pre-drawn graph axes** on graph paper are similar. Again, drawing graph axes with the appropriate scales is an important skill. However, some students will find this so hard that they are not then able to engage with the meaning of the graph . . . they are still sweating it out, getting the numbers to fit on their axes. If the analysis of the graph is the main learning point, it pays to have some ready-made graphs that students can plot straight on to.

- **Writing frames** for writing up experiments and investigations. In good departments, you should have writing frames with decreasing levels of support. The weakest students may have some sense of what their results show, but putting it into writing is tough, and they often don't know where to start – so show them. For example:

  > The aim of the experiment is to explore the relationship between . . . and . . .
  >
  > Our hypothesis is that the . . . will double if . . .
  >
  > The graph shows that . . . increases/decreases as . . . increases.
  >
  > I predicted that, if the concentration of acid was doubled, then . . .
  >
  > In conclusion, the results of our experiment show that . . .

A similar approach can be applied to the instructions for tasks – either experiments or research tasks. These may need to be prepared for a specific topic, but the idea is to give students of different abilities an appropriate level of guidance. For example:

- No support:

  Research the issue of nuclear power and prepare a case study of the construction of a new power station, with a clear conclusion.

- More support:

  Identify the key advantages of nuclear power and the key disadvantages.

  Consider the environmental impact on people and wildlife living in the area.

  Consider the benefits to people in the country in terms of the supply of electricity.

  Write a short paragraph giving the case for each side of the argument.

  Write your own conclusion.

- **Writing frame**: You may have students who would need a specific structure prepared for this specific task, outlining the key words, the paragraph structure and sentence starters.

ACTIVITY

Produce a writing frame that gives lower-ability students a good framework to answer standard 'advantages and disadvantages' questions, such as in relation to building a hydroelectric dam, or comparing organic pesticides with chemical pesticides. Include sentence starters and paragraph structure guidance.

Different tasks

'**Differentiation by outcome**' is where the same stimulus leads to open-ended responses, allowing students to operate at a level of challenge appropriate for their ability. In science, this is usually achieved by setting out a series of tasks or questions of increasing difficulty, so that students can work at the appropriate level. In the spirit of 'teaching to the top', the main thrust of this must be to ensure the ablest students are fully challenged.

The key variable in outcomes will be the depth of answer – the sophistication of the explanations given, the quality of a presentation, the rigour of the analysis of some data. Good formative assessment strategies (see Chapter 8) will help to guide this process, using effective success criteria and exemplars.

In practical work, the outcomes can be very different. Students may focus on one variable, seeking to gain one good set of results, while others could be exploring multiple variables and seeking to compare two relationships. Students can be given different levels of freedom to design or adapt their own experiments.

Completely different tasks can be set if necessary, but this is complicated. In some scenarios, you may have a group engaging in self-supported extended study or practical work, while others are working on questions at a more basic level. Or it could be that students work on completely different questions, from different sources, that are tailored for their reading ability. The challenge here is to bring the students back together to tease out common learning, so that you retain the whole-class dynamic. It is very hard to sustain completely separate pathways for multiple lessons within one class. Avoid doing that, if you can.

Different questions

Some textbooks or worksheets provide excellent self-levelling question series. Students tackle questions of increasing difficulty, self-checking answers against a mark scheme, and, therefore, move at different rates. It is often necessary to direct students to tackle appropriate questions, making sure the more able students don't necessarily have to wade through the easier material before they tackle the more challenging questions.

> In biology GCSE, students are presented with a range of questions on cards.
>
> The tiered questions are identified as bronze, silver or gold. Depending on confidence and success, students are able to self-select the questions they want to tackle, using prepared answers to self-check. The students need to produce several correct answers within one level before moving on. The teacher prompts some students to move on faster and suggests to others that they consolidate.

Inclusive questioning: this is the teacher's great skill: to bring all students in a class into a question and answer exchange, adjusting the level of questioning to the student in a subtle way. Mini-whiteboards are brilliant for this. As I describe in Chapter 6, the whiteboards allow you to field multiple answers to the same questions.

A key aspect of differentiation in questioning is to reinforce your expectations of students' oral responses, supporting literacy development. A good process is to ask for answers from named individuals, accept their first rough attempt, but to then ask for a more coherent version.

> In a chemistry lesson on electrolysis:
>
> *Teacher:* So, what is happening at the negative electrode?
> *Student:* Bubbles of hydrogen.
>
> Now, depending on the student, the follow-up might be:

Planning for differentiation

> *Teacher:* Yes, that's correct; but can you put that into a
> sentence for me?
> *Student:* Bubbles of hydrogen gas are being produced at the
> negative electrode.
>
> *Or,* for a more able student:
>
> *Teacher:* OK, that's correct, but can you give me a more
> detailed explanation in terms of ions and electrons?
> *Student:* The positive hydrogen ions are attracted to the
> negative electrode, gaining electrons and forming hydrogen
> molecules that then collect into bubbles.
>
> In both cases, the student is being pushed further, their use of
> language or oral literacy is being developed, and they both
> could form part of a whole-class discussion. Everyone is
> engaged; everyone is challenged. That's the idea.

Different grouping strategies

A range of grouping strategies can be adopted to facilitate differentiated learning. An overriding consideration is to seek to ensure that
the grouping increases students' capacity to learn, rather than
providing them with an opportunity to hide.

Leadership grouping: more able students are given leadership
responsibility in mixed-ability groups, with a 'group goal' that
requires any group member to report back. Each group member
may have an allocated task, but they all share the collective goals.
This arrangement leads to good discussions, peer instruction and
peer negotiation, as a shared response is demanded.

Paired tutoring or students as teachers: here, pairs are set up
where the role of one student is to instruct the other. Students of
differing ability are in each pair; they can swap roles, provide support and challenge, as they try to construct coherent explanations
or solve problems.

Grouping by ability with different tasks or questions: as part of the variety of groupings, you can group by ability, so that the ablest students have an opportunity to work together, while you focus support on groupings of lower-ability students together. The tasks normally need to vary here. This works well with practical work, where the extent of the instructions given or freedom to devise the experiments can be very different.

Experts groups: this is an excellent strategy that is worth setting up from time to time.

ENERGY CRISIS EXPERT PANEL

A Year 9 class exploring energy sources is divided into six expert groups: wind, nuclear, coal, solar, hydroelectric and gas. Each group of four or five students researches their particular energy source to find out the key benefits and costs. The class is then reconfigured into five groups, each comprising one person from each of the expert groups. They are now expert panels. The goal of each group is to share the information, in order to plan an energy strategy for a particular location. Each group may have a different location, so that there is no one correct answer.

Making differentiation explicit and routine

The key to success with differentiation is to create an environment where the language of differentiation permeates every lesson. I am not advocating that you write differentiated learning objectives slavishly on the board, but it should be clear that there are various learning goals that different students should be aiming for. An effective teacher will cut to the chase, anticipating that certain students will need to push forward or need support, right from the start of any activity that demands it. At other times, it is sensible and desirable to see how your students get on with a core activity, before they diverge. This requires some routines that you should establish with your classes:

Which groups are we in today?

To make groupings easy to manage and routine, it is helpful to have codes for the variants.

You might want everyone in their planet groups – this could mean that Venus is the more able group, and Mars is the group that needs additional support. You might want everyone in their animal groups, and reptiles and mammals might just be parallel, mixed-ability groups. You could, of course, just use colours, letters, numbers or shapes.

What do we do if we don't know what to do?

Teaching self-help learning strategies is a vital tool in the kit. Students should learn that there are various sources of help: They can think for themselves. They can ask a friend for help: peer support is a very helpful aspect of mixed-ability teaching. They can also check the instructions or the information in the book. It is astonishing how often students do not read instructions . . . they look at them, but default to asking the teacher regardless, unless encouraged not to.

If these things are reinforced, there is less 'Miss, I'm stuck' or 'Sir, can you help?' to deal with. In lessons with fifteen Bunsen burners, twelve electrical circuits or twenty titrations going on, this is going to make a big difference.

What do we do if we've finished?

Ideally, you should set your lessons up in advance so that there is no such thing as 'finished'. In very effective lessons, you never see students waiting, hands up or killing time, with nothing to do.

So, in setting up the lesson, make this aspect crystal clear: 'Do A, then B, and, if you have finished, there is always C or D . . .'

More subtly, your classroom culture should encourage students to push on to the next level, if they're finding the work easy. Great teachers fuel this 'can do' spirit that gives students confidence to get into the deep end at every opportunity.

I think it is legitimate, and even necessary, to give students a degree of ownership and responsibility for directing their learning in terms of the level of challenge. You need to create the opportunities, but your students need to learn that, ultimately, it is up to them to find their level. Encourage them not to suffer in silence, but also urge them not to coast. They need to do their bit.

In this area, you do also need to give consideration to students' self-esteem. It can hold a student back to know they are always in the low-ability group. At the same time, the issue of ability can't be tiptoed around. Students see through any attempt to mask it. Again, it comes down to culture. Mixing up the groupings over time, using a range of differentiation strategies and creating a general deep-end, high-challenge spirit are needed; knowing how students deal with this on the self-esteem scale is part of your knowledge bank, just as much as their data targets.

The spirit of differentiation

In my experience, the best lessons are characterised by teaching and learning where differentiation is integral to the entire process, where the notion that one size does not fit all and that different learners will be progressing at different rates is absolutely explicit and embedded.

On the surface, differentiation may appear to be a series of concrete strategies. However, to my mind, this is much the same as suggesting that an artist or footballer has style or flair, at the same time as being able to analyse what specific skills they employ. It is the blending of those skills that leads to the overall impact; this is the 'spirit of differentiation'.

Planning for differentiation

Where differentiation is embedded, it can't fall off the edge; you don't forget to differentiate – it simply happens all the time, because that is how you think as a teacher.

Differentiation is a habit. To begin with, you need to work on each strategy to build up your repertoire, but, ultimately, it is something you do every day, without thinking.

TALKING POINTS

1   What does a 'total philosophy of gifted and talented provision' look like in practice?
2   How do we avoid the 'fixed mindset' problem of labelling students as 'able' or 'less able' leading to a self-fulfilling prophecy, defeatism or complacency? Should we use these terms at all?
3   Which differentiation strategies require special preparation, and what can you do every day, every lesson, all the time?

5 Managing behaviour and building relationships

One of the core joys of teaching is the process of forming relationships with students. As well as being highly rewarding in itself, this is a prerequisite for effective teaching. It is also one of the most challenging aspects of becoming a great teacher, because it's easy to get it wrong.

I've observed hundreds of different teachers who have had excellent classroom management skills; each of them has been an individual, with a unique personality. To some extent, every teacher manages their classroom and their relationships with students in their own way; sometimes, this can be highly idiosyncratic.

I once worked with Alison, who addressed her most truculent Year 9s with, 'Lovely to see you darlings; Nathan, sweetheart, could you sit over here for me, gorgeous. Sophie, let's have that work out now, lovely'. This was how she spoke to everyone; she had them eating out of her hand. The lessons were challenging, and, behind the effusively positive language, there was steel: nobody messed with Alison. All it took was a disapproving look and an occasional, 'Er . . . Michael my lovely, this way please', and they fell obligingly back into line.

Clearly, that isn't a reproducible strategy. We can't all be Alison, even if we wanted to.

There are, however, some common elements to effective behaviour management that can be learned, practised and improved on, so that it is possible to work confidently with any class and any student. Essentially, it comes down to a few things. A student's perspective might be this:

- The teacher can control the class – students know what is expected, and where the boundaries are.
- The teacher is on your side – there are positive relationships and mutual respect.
- The teacher is fair – everyone is treated within a justice framework that is clearly understood.

Positive relationships

An essential starting point when developing behaviour management skills is to adopt a philosophy based on positive regard for the young people in your class. The same power and opportunity that you have to inspire and enthuse your students, lighting fires of ambition and curiosity, give you the power to crush a young person's self-esteem or turn them off science altogether.

Positive behaviour management starts with a view of each member of your class as an individual, whose feelings and ambitions as a person matter as much to them as their understanding of science. Each member of a class has value as a person; you are there to teach science to Sabrina, Jack, Daisy, Sam, Harun and Alicia, not just to teach science to a generic class of empty vessels, with no personality or character.

As we've said previously, it is not your teaching that matters in the end; it is the learning of the specific young people in your care.

For some, this is a key reason to be a teacher in the first place. It comes naturally to seek out warm, positive, friendly relationships with students, based on mutual respect. For others, this is more difficult. The goal is to find an appropriate balance between being kind, caring, friendly and approachable, and retaining a professional distance and calm authority that is non-negotiable.

Teaching and parenting have a lot in common. Effective parenting normally includes conveying unconditional love and providing a safe, nurturing environment while also communicating very clear boundaries, backed with the authority of enforcement.

Of course, although you may question the motives of some people for joining the profession, it is possible to teach while being fairly cool or indifferent to your students as people; you certainly don't need to be a touchy-feely sort of person. There are actually plenty of pitfalls in being over-familiar and matey. You are not there to be anyone's friend, and it never pays to court popularity for its own sake.

At the same time, you are also much less likely to succeed in establishing and sustaining a strongly effective learning environment with a class if you reinforce an inflexible authoritarian culture, show contempt or active disregard for individuals' feelings or fuel conflict. As with parenting, you are the adult, you are the grown-up – which is important to remember when you're challenged and your emotions kick in.

In the very best learning situations, the relationships between the students and teacher are strongly positive. There is a warm rapport, and the teacher knows the students as individuals. Mutual respect has built up over time, and everyone knows the boundaries, and this all leads to a joyfulness in the learning process, even when the going is getting tough, because you're all in it together.

Assertiveness

Being assertive is the bedrock of effective behaviour management. An assertive teacher will address the class with confidence, with a firm, direct tone of voice, making plenty of eye contact with students around the room and commanding the space. An assertive teacher will also assume authority where behaviour needs to be corrected or challenged, addressing the situation with certainty and assurance, expecting compliance and insisting on it.

Managing behaviour and building relationships

A teacher who is not assertive enough might do these things:

- convey a lack of confidence through a meek tone of voice or body language;

- appear timid or hesitant when calling a class to attention or asking questions;

- allow students to talk while the teacher is talking, or to not face towards the teacher;

- appear apologetic in challenging any off-task behaviour, pleading for compliance, conveying a lack of belief that students will respond;

- remain fixed in their position in a classroom, thereby not appearing to be at ease in the whole space;

- avoid eye contact, conveying a fear of direct interaction;

- be reluctant to approach or challenge more truculent, defiant individuals;

- issue corrective instructions, but not follow up if they are not complied with.

The goal, then, is to develop the skills so that you do not do these things. Confidence is key, and that really only develops organically over time, but you can learn to project an assertive demeanour, even if you don't feel particularly assertive inside. There are four key elements to appearing assertive, each of which can be rehearsed:

- confident body language: standing tall, facing the class, using your hands;

- eye-contact: talking and looking directly at students and expecting the same from them;

- owning the space: using the whole space to assert authority, talking from various positions around the room, walking up and down the line or around any space;

- authoritative tone of voice: clear and strong in tone, conveying certainty about any instructions.

> **ACTIVITY**
>
> If you find these things difficult, take time to practise them, much as you might do in a drama class. With a trusted colleague or a video camera to provide feedback, find a moment to act out the 'assertive teacher' role and work on the areas you need to.

Gaining attention

There are lots of situations in science lessons where there is a need to gain the full attention of every member of a class, with them all listening to you or to someone in the group, facing forwards and taking heed of what is being said.

This could be the start of a lesson, after the students have arrived from elsewhere. It could be after you've asked a question and engaged them all in lively debate in pairs. It could be partway through a practical session, where you need to issue some precise instructions or address a safety issue.

In each of these situations, it is important to recognise that the best-behaved, most conscientious students have perfectly natural and legitimate tendencies to want to continue with what they are doing, rather than to listen to you.

If you ever follow a group of students around for the day, you realise that the social bubble they inhabit is extraordinarily strong. They are in a world where the dominant aspect is being together – drifting from French to maths to music and then to science. The subject context is often secondary, and it takes time to disconnect from simultaneous equations or the future conditional to begin thinking about mitochondria and respiration. It also takes a little time to stop thinking about the hilarious joke John just told, in the corridor.

Similarly, if you've just asked a really great question ('How would life be different if the strength of gravity fell by 50%?' 'Would you eat a genetically modified chicken burger?'), or you've got everyone excited by getting their apparatus set up (they are about to grow their own crystals or plant their own seeds for the first time), it's not entirely surprising that they're reluctant to stop to listen to you in an instant.

At times, it can feel as if you're facing a wall of indifference, or that you are herding cats ... successfully gathering some, while losing others. This can be demoralising, if you allow it to be.

However, rather than seeing this as a surprise or irritating, or assuming that they are acting defiantly or disrespectfully, you need to develop systems for gaining attention that assume students are acting perfectly naturally and normally.

There are a number of approaches you might try, and you may well use all of them at different phases of a lesson.

1 **Slowly reel them in**: This is the patient approach. You issue an instruction, asking for attention, using a firm, assertive voice, and gather everyone together, using eye contact, scanning the room, giving them time to get out of their bubble and into yours. At the same time, you offer affirming praise, verbally or non-verbally, to those doing what you've asked.

> 'OK, 9S, let's have you all listening and facing the front thanks.'
> (Pause)
> 'Thanks John, Michaela, that's perfect ... just waiting for the others.'
> 'Nearly there ...'
> 'Clara? Alex? ... (gain eye contact) ... Brilliant. We're all ready.'

Using names and giving time is the key here. It is positive and relaxed, but your expectations are absolutely clear and definite. Students will know that they have some leeway, but not much.

2   **Use a defined signal**: This could be a silent raised arm – which, perhaps, they also have to copy; a countdown ('Three, two, one. Everyone listening'); it could be a sound: a double clap, three taps with a pen on the whiteboard, a shaker, a handbell, taps on a cup (the classic speech-making signal) or very simply a loud verbal command: '*And stop*'.

Early on, you need to rehearse this signal and then enforce it routinely, lesson after lesson. The expectations need to be clear. This is the signal. It means 'Stop talking, face the front and listen.' The consequences of not following the signal need to be spelled out. Don't use a signal half-heartedly. Use it often or not at all; whenever necessary, re-establish and rehearse it, so that students know you mean it.

With most signals, you also need an engagement pause: Give the signal. Pause for full engagement . . . and then affirm. 'Thanks, that's great.' If necessary, rein in the stragglers, without too much drama in the first instance. Reserve dishing out consequences for persistence rather than borderline infringements, taking care to be consistent over time.

In a lot of practical lessons, it is very important to have a well-understood safety stop signal that means: 'Stop! Stand still and listen *now!*' This could be because of broken glass, something on fire, a chemical spill or any other hazard. A loud '*freeze*' is often very effective, provided that you only use it for this purpose.

3   **Use time indicators**: It can be effective to set time limits for various episodes in a lesson, setting the expectation that, by the end of this time, students will be sitting down, facing front, listening and ready. This could be on entry to the classroom: 'OK, 7S, in you come, 60 seconds to be ready and listening.'

It could be during a questioning sequence: 'In your pairs, discuss (why does the compound change colour when we heat it?) . . . two minutes'. Then simply count down near the end.

It could be in the set-up phase of a practical: 'Right, you know where everything is; you've got five minutes to gather the apparatus, set it up and be ready with your results table open'.

Once you set up the expectation of a time limit, students will accept and anticipate the countdown to stop and, if you create the right atmosphere, will seek to gain your approval by meeting the target.

Sustaining attention

Arguably, this is the most difficult skill to master, and it probably requires the most practice and experience. The biggest difficulty with gaining attention, in order to engage in the various learning modes, is that, from time to time, some students will inevitably drop out of your whole-class bubble and switch back into their personal one. To a great extent, this is human nature; for many people, their immediate desire on having a thought is to share it with someone. Often, they lose concentration unknowingly and drift off. It can appear rude, but it may not be deliberate. Adults do this all the time; it is all too common for teachers to whisper at the back of meetings or even around a small table.

It is essential, therefore, to anticipate this tendency and to establish clear expectations that, once students have been called to attention to listen, talking is not permitted – and that includes whispering, *even if it is about the work*. Students should raise a hand to ask a question or use some other agreed protocol.

With that expectation clearly stated, the challenge is to maintain a vigilant overview of students' engagement and to redirect students who have strayed into off-task talking. You should never continue to talk if you have asked for full attention and some students are not paying attention.

If you know it is Alicia who is talking, address her directly, giving her time to respond: (Pause) 'Alicia . . . [secure eye contact]. Thanks, I want you listening and facing me. That's great.' Then continue.

If you detect talking but cannot pinpoint the sources, then make a general comment, aiming your gaze in the general direction. 'OK ... [pause ... scan] ... let's have everyone focused and listening. [Pause for engagement] Thanks.' Simply pausing can give the message you want to give.

I'd suggest that the most common features of lessons where behaviour management is poor are that students talk too freely, regardless of whether the teacher is talking, and they are not challenged consistently, if at all. It can take time to develop the teacher radar and peripheral vision needed to pick up every transgression as you talk or write on the board, but that's the challenge.

Certainly, if faced with repeated failures to listen, you must use the range of consequences described later in the chapter. However, if you allow off-task talking to continue, in the students' eyes you are basically condoning it, and that is what some of them will do. It then becomes harder to challenge later.

In the longer term, once you've established your credentials as someone who is assertive and will follow up with consequences, holding attention is a matter of continual scanning, holding eye contact as you talk, pausing occasionally to make redirecting commands or gestures, and insisting on compliance when necessary.

In my experience, even with the most wonderful class of well-behaved students you can imagine, you never reach a point where this becomes unnecessary. It is always necessary to reinforce expectations around talking and listening.

Expectations and routines

Another key ingredient in developing a successful repertoire of behaviour management strategies is to tie your expectations into routines. This makes it easier to establish your expectations, to reinforce them over time and to avoid creating an endless list of ad hoc rules.

As far as possible, you should follow the agreed, whole-school policy on this, so that, when students come to your class, you are merely reinforcing messages that your colleagues are giving around the school. It rarely pays dividends to be more lenient or stricter than the rest.

However, you also need to blend the whole-school rules with those pertinent to your space and the requirements of science lessons. Some of the routines you need to think about include the following:

- When entering the class and getting started, do they go in and stand behind chairs in silence? Do they go straight in, get all of their equipment out and sit down ready and listening? What happens when you take the register? What should they call you?

- When engaging in written work, how do they set it out? How do you want them to use their exercise books? Are there rules and expectations about using a pen for writing and a pencil for diagrams? Are there consequences for failing to bring in basic equipment? If work is due to be handed in, what are the routines for collecting it in?

- When working individually, do you want silence, or is quiet talking permitted? Don't ask for 'silence' and then permit talking. If you want silence, say what you mean and insist on it.

- When you are writing on the board, do you want them listening, pens down, or are they allowed or even expected to make notes?

- What is the procedure for getting practical work started and packing away the apparatus afterwards? For example, do you have monitors or volunteers, or does everyone do their own?

- What are the routines for getting into groups, moving around the classroom for a front-bench demo, and asking or answering questions?

- What is the standard procedure if students ask permission to go to the toilet, to go to music lessons, ask for a drink of water, have a nosebleed or complain of period pain?

- How should students be dismissed? Row by row, or by some other system? Do they stand up behind chairs first? Do you insist on silence first?

Importantly, you also need to turn your expectations around gaining attention into routines, so they are well rehearsed, and you have the confidence to plan the learning in the way you want to. For example, in order to engage in effective, dynamic question and answer sessions, you need good stop–start routines.

The more of this you do, the easier it becomes. From time to time, you can revisit the rules and rehearse them, as needed. It is often useful to do this at the start of a new term. With classes that you find particularly difficult, you may occasionally need to focus on these routines explicitly, at the expense of teaching content, simply to restate your expectations and reinforce your authority. Don't be afraid to do this if you are not happy; it pays off in the end.

Finally, remember this: if you are not happy with the behaviour in your lessons at any point, tackle it. Any behaviour that is unchallenged will become routine, unless you do something to change it.

ACTIVITY

Work out your answer to all the questions posed above. Think about how you will explain them to the students you teach, without it seeming like a very long list of rules. Rehearse these routines with your classes very clearly and explicitly, repeating as necessary, until you are getting the response you want.

Using language for effect

Inspired by the work of Bill Rogers, I have found that it is extremely powerful to develop a mode of teacher talk where my use of language reinforces the more overt messages I am trying to give.

This can be artificial at first, but, with practice, it soon becomes habitual. There are two main areas that I find useful.

Affirmative language

Here, when giving commands, you focus on the outcomes you want, rather than the opposite. Here are some examples:

- 'I'd like the back table facing forwards with books open and equipment ready. Thank you.'

- 'Hassan, I want that retort stand back in the rack and your books all packed away in your bag.'

- 'Sadiq [pause for attention], this is a silent study task. Thanks. First warning.'

- 'Matthew and Jamie, I'd like all five questions answered before you go to lunch. OK? Thanks.'

- 'Rohini. What's our rule about walking around the lab? Let's stick to it thanks. Great.'

The effect is powerful. Instead of a stream of corrective negatives, you convey the message, while maintaining a positive atmosphere and avoiding conflict. If you tell a student that you want them listening in silence, the effect is different from asking them to stop talking. You give them space, the benefit of the doubt, and reinforce what you want, rather than what you don't want.

Similarly, it often pays dividends to focus on students who are doing what you want, rather than give attention to those who are not:

- 'Well done to this table. We're all focused on the graph and trying to plot the points accurately.'

- 'Superb work James. That's set up just right and you've got your safety glasses on ready to go.'

- 'Thanks to this row here. Everyone appears to be listening and ready.'

- 'We've got a superb collection of homework here; these students will get the feedback next lesson.'

By concentrating on the actions of compliant students, you get things in perspective. Instead of berating the three latecomers, you thank the twenty-five who arrived on time. The message is clear, but the emphasis is different. This also works for homework, listening, packing away and any number of other tasks and expectations.

The language of choice

There are many situations where you achieve a swift, positive outcome with students who are not behaving well by offering a choice, rather than focusing on a specific demand. If you develop a language of choice in your everyday dealings with students, it creates a culture where students learn to make decisions about their behaviour, without feeling boxed into a corner. Usually, the choice is between doing what you want them to do now, or doing something they'll find less palatable that has the same outcome.

- 'You can finish the work now, or stay on at lunch and do it then.'

- 'You can sit by yourself where I've asked you to, or work silently where you are now.'

- 'You can do the experiment sensibly on your own, or I can join you and we can do it together.'

- 'You can listen as I've asked, or I can give you a formal warning and log it on the system.'

Students will not always make the right choice, but, very often, they will, if you give them one. If they don't, you must follow through with the alternative, without exception. I have found this strategy incredibly helpful in the classroom, and it has been helpful at home with my children too.

ACTIVITY

Practise using affirmative language and language of choice. Try it out with a colleague, for a bit of fun, but then test it out for real in a class. It becomes natural after a while, but keep practising until it does.

Individuals and group dynamics

Traditional school environments place young people into social scenarios that most adults do not have to contend with day to day. Learning science in a class of twenty or thirty places students in a situation where group dynamics and peer pressure will play a part, and it is helpful and healthy to develop an awareness of how these things manifest themselves.

Firstly, you should not lose sight of the fact that each teaching group is comprised of individuals. It is natural enough for you to think about teaching 9S, 7Y or your Year 11 GCSE class at a broad planning level. However, when managing behaviour, you need to avoid falling into the trap of attributing the behaviour of individuals to the whole class.

Sadly, some teachers do this too often and say things like: '7D is an awful class'; 'they are a nightmare to teach'; 'everyone is being too noisy'; 'they never do any homework'; '9H never concentrate for more than 5 minutes'.

These generalisations are highly toxic and don't actually help to resolve issues. Although it may feel as if an entire class is failing to listen, is talking noisily, has low expectations regarding the outcomes expected, is late, has arrived without the equipment . . . it is highly unlikely to be true. All group behaviours are the sum of individual behaviours, and, in most cases, it is only a minority of students who create the problems you face in establishing the learning atmosphere you want.

Secondly, take account of the power of peer pressure. It is difficult for some students to abstain from the negative behaviours their friends have engaged in. Some students crave attention; they regularly look for an audience to build their self-esteem. Other students are too ready to encourage someone else to be the clown for their entertainment. Some students will do anything to avoid losing face in front of their peers and can be deeply affected by the experience of feeling publicly humiliated or 'shown up'. It is a deeply established taboo in many peer group settings to 'dob someone in' or 'grass them up', because of the consequences of months of aggravation afterwards.

Although you may wish to get in among the group to challenge these dynamics, often you simply need to work with them. Some approaches to consider include the following:

- Try to deal with as many issues as possible on an individual basis. Analyse the dynamics in your class and tackle the students who are the source of the problems.

- Avoid generalised negative language about the class; think about individuals and address the issues with individuals during lessons. Challenge five or ten people talking, rather than yell at the whole class.

- Even if multiple students are behaving poorly, keep perspective, affirming the behaviour of those who are doing what you want with praise and thanks.

- Generate seating arrangements that break up negative peer dynamics within the class and reinforce positive ones. Take time to explain this to students and give them the opportunity to redeem themselves over time.

- Set high expectations concerning any form of language that might diminish the self-esteem of other students: it should never be acceptable for students to be laughed at for getting answers wrong or for being too clever.

- Avoid engaging in public confrontations where face-saving will be an issue. Use the space in a room – or use support systems – to take a student out of the public gaze, so that issues can be resolved with the heat taken out of them and without the drama of a public showdown.

- You should never use sarcastic or personal language to challenge a student, but this is especially true in a whole-class situation. If you do, you lose their respect and the respect of the whole class. Students are often loyal to each other and, although they want you to keep order, they won't stand for injustice.

Consequences and systems

Every school will have a system for reinforcing good behaviour, with a set of established consequences that follow when students fall short of expectations. It is beyond the scope of this book to describe all the variants of whole-school systems, but you can assume that there will be a set of procedures set out for all staff to follow, communicated to parents and students.

The value of a good system of consequences is that it should empower you to manage behaviour such that, to the greatest possible extent, the consequences are not actually needed, because you secure the behaviour you want. To achieve this, you need to use the language of choice explicitly, reinforced continually:

- 'Clara, I am giving you a warning. You can listen as I've asked or I will report your behaviour on the system.'

- 'Sam, what will happen if you choose to call out again?' The rules are known, and the consequences are well understood. It is a rhetorical question.

The ultimate goal, as far as possible, is to create the circumstances where students are effectively choosing to be punished in some way because of their behaviour choices, rather than having sanctions imposed punitively and retrospectively, based on warnings given long ago, or rule statements that are rarely articulated. You are not trying to catch them out – you want them not to misbehave in the first place.

Essentially, there are three levels of sanction that you might need to engage with.

Classroom sanctions

Verbal admonishments

This might be obvious, but what might simply be called 'telling someone off' is by far the most effective form of sanction in most situations. Most students will adjust their behaviour so that they do not get told off. If you have a form of assertive language to convey a very firm message that says, 'you have seriously disappointed me and I won't tolerate it', while also suggesting that you still care and hold the student in high regard, you almost don't need anything more.

This is not the same as shouting or giving a dressing down. It is the measured, disciplined voice of a grown-up, albeit with a tinge of severity in your language. My default, first-base sanction of this kind is to say something like this: 'If you continue to do that, despite being asked very politely, I will be very cross indeed'. Because they have seen what 'cross' looks like, that is normally sufficient warning. Then, I step back down into my normal, friendly mode.

Formal warnings

Very often, whole-school systems are based on incremental warnings that then lead to further sanctions if the warnings are not heeded. The key here is to make it very explicit that a formal warning has been given. They may be given a name – a 'strike' or a 'C1' – depending on the system. It may involve noting the student's name on the board or logging it on a system.

You must use these systems to support you; if you dish out the warnings like confetti, you devalue them instantly. If you get angry a lot, but do not use the system, you're not helping yourself. Be as consistent as you can and follow up with the next level of sanctions, if that is what the student's behaviour dictates.

Classroom restrictions

Within the flow of a lesson, you can often use a particular space, usually near your own work area, to signify an area of maximum supervision, moving students to sit there as a consequence. Alternatively, you can move students around the room for similar effect, again, having given a clear choice in advance.

With practical lessons, where safety concerns are critical, there is always the option to withdraw participation in the practical activity. However, this must be used sparingly; it should be a serious sanction, because the practical work is part of the learning. I urge you not to be the kind of science teacher who says, 'we're not doing practical work because you're being too noisy', denying every individual a core learning experience because of the unrelated poor behaviour of a minority. Using practical work as a carrot to secure compliance is problematic, so be careful in going down this path.

Sending out

In some schools, sending students out into the corridor is routine, using momentary exclusion of this kind as a pragmatic cooling-off process. In other schools, this is not accepted, for various reasons. If there is a 'sending out' option, you must ensure that you do not leave the student unsupervised for more than a few moments, and, if you go outside to talk to them, you must be sure that the class can continue to work safely and calmly. The warnings ahead of a sending out must be absolutely unequivocal, and, unless the student then redeems him- or herself, there should normally be a follow-up punitive sanction, to underline the severity of the situation.

The verbal 'electric fence'

Perhaps the ultimate classroom sanction, which many teachers keep in reserve, is a very sharp, severe but controlled angry voice that expresses maximum displeasure but also total authority, without suggesting a loss of control. If you do have cause to use this mode of communication, students will remember and they won't want to see it too often. You are basically saying, 'Do Not Ever Do That Again', in no uncertain terms.

Not every teacher can do this, or wants to. For some, it spills over into a genuine loss of control that can be destructive for all concerned. However, if pushed, the occasional zap from the electric fence can be very powerful in showing where the boundary lies, allowing a very relaxed and friendly environment to thrive within it. Obviously, if you overuse this method, you diminish the effect, but be prepared to reinforce your expectations very firmly, if you need to.

ACTIVITY

Test out your verbal 'electric fence'. How cross can you sound without actually being angry? Act out your 'strict teacher' voice in a private space, but then try to use it when you are faced with a situation that requires you to gain control immediately.

School-level sanctions

Most schools will have a system for detentions – within a department, year group or for the whole school – a system for on-call removal of disruptive students, protocols for students to be parked in the classroom of a colleague and a variety of reporting systems to enlist the support of pastoral or senior staff. You may also set your own detentions and sanctions.

The obvious advice is to learn what your options are and then to use them on a sliding scale as you need, to help reinforce good behaviour in your classroom. These systems are there to support you, and, if you use them in a measured, consistent manner, you can use them to lever up the standard of behaviour in your lessons, while retaining full authority.

If you feel there is chaos in your lesson, where the disruptive behaviour of any number of students is unacceptable and beyond your control, you must call for support. This may involve sending a student to a designated point or the use of a computer or telephone system.

Teacher: OK. This behaviour is completely unacceptable. If it continues, I will need to call the on-call teacher.

(The behaviour continues.)

Teacher: Right. That is the choice you've made . . . (action the on-call system).

By adopting this approach, where you take ownership of the decision, you retain the position of authority. When the on-call teacher arrives, you can then request removal or support in reinforcing the expectations; try not to defer to the person when they arrive. Stand with them and act in unison.

In contrast, if you struggle bravely to no avail, leading to the alarm being raised owing to noise levels, and a senior member of staff arrives at your door unexpectedly, you may lose some credibility. Whenever possible, try to be the person making the decisions, following up with the consequences and taking ownership of the process.

If, for example, there is a whole-school or departmental detention you can put students in, it pays to go along yourself at the beginning, so that the students see you have followed up and are in control of the process.

Above all, with sanctions of this kind, avoid making empty threats. Don't threaten a detention and then never give one; don't set a detention and then forget about it or cancel it, half-heartedly. Use warnings, escalate through all the in-class sanctions, give students the option to redeem themselves, and use the sanctions firmly and clearly if they continue to make the bad choices that take you down that path.

Formal disciplinary procedures

I am including these for completeness. All schools will have disciplinary procedures that will include the possibility of internal exclusions or isolations and fixed-term exclusions, where students attend off-site units or stay at home for a number of days.

As a classroom teacher, you should operate in the knowledge that these systems are there to support you. However, they are complex and, most often, they are enacted at a level that you do not engage with directly, except by providing written statements about specific incidents.

Once you get to know your school, you will get a sense of the scale of behaviour issues and the likelihood of exclusions of one kind or another being deployed. It is important not to get involved in making threats about exclusion, even in extreme cases, because this can put you and other staff in a difficult position later on. You must allow the people charged with responsibility for disciplinary procedures to make a judgement, based on the information they receive.

There will be a process for reporting issues, and you must use this robustly. It is usually very helpful to talk to a senior colleague about a serious incident, before writing a statement. A personal report often conveys the nuances of a situation more effectively than an email or statement written while in an emotional state.

ACTIVITY

Before you start teaching in any situation, make sure you know what the basic school rules are, and what the system is for getting help if you need it. Read the school behaviour policy and make sure you know the terminology and how the systems work.

Conflict resolution

From time to time, you may encounter a situation where a student or a group of students appears to be acting in open defiance of your authority. They may flatly deny any wrongdoing, refuse to cooperate with instructions or engage in a dispute about your interpretation of their behaviour.

As far as you possibly can, try to diffuse conflict by seeking a middle path in your everyday interactions with students. You do not have to have the last word; you don't need to be absolutely beyond question, in order to retain your authority. In fact, the opposite is often true:

Teacher: Jason, could you get on with your work please. I'd like you to finish questions 4 and 5.

Jason: But I wasn't doing anything Sir. I wasn't even talking. I'm doing my work.

Teacher: OK, maybe you were. That's great. Let's see your answers in a few minutes.

Or:

Teacher: Ayo, that was your final warning, I now want you to move up next to me as I asked.

Ayo: No Sir. It wasn't me. I didn't do anything. I'm not moving.

Teacher: OK ... maybe not, but it would be better if you moved now, so we can get settled and move on.

Ayo: That's not fair Sir.

Teacher: OK, that's your view but I'd like you to move now so you can show me some decent work without being distracted. Or, if you like, you can work next door with Mrs Campbell. Which would you prefer?

Ultimately, the negotiations have to stop – there is a bottom line, where your judgement is the one that matters, and your decisions are absolute. However, as these exchanges illustrate, you can still work with students to bring them with you, giving them ways to come back around and avoiding conflict. Meeting partway is a vital strategy.

Sometimes, however, relationships do break down. You may feel you have an irredeemably poor rapport with a whole class, or persistent conflict with a student, despite trying various approaches, both hard and soft. If you get into this situation, you must engage the support of a colleague to map out a strategy to restore working relationships and regain trust and respect from all parties.

Some of these approaches might include the following:

- A one-to-one meeting with a student to talk through the issues, away from their peers: This might be mediated by a member of the pastoral staff. You may also involve parents. If you can make a connection with a student in a new, more personal context, it can help massively when you see them back in class. It could be a small group of students. You may agree some form of contract and a monitoring period, after which the situation would be reviewed.

- A planned withdrawal of one or more individuals from a class: With support from a colleague, it can pay to re-establish a positive relationship with a class while the more recalcitrant members are withdrawn for a few lessons, prior to reintegrating them. All of this would be done with the parents' knowledge.

- A relaunch: It can pay dividends to enlist the support of a senior colleague to re-establish all the basic expectations and routines: lining up, entering the room, listening, asking questions, working quietly, following instructions . . . the whole lot. A fresh start can do wonders, and you can choose to do that at almost any time.

It is supremely powerful in these processes to adopt an explicit resolution-seeking approach. If you see the processes as ways to demonstrate your absolute authority, then you won't get too far. It is a learning process for the students concerned, where you can set out clear expectations while also giving them a voice about the difficulties they experience.

Emotional well-being

Finally, I feel it is important to recognise that managing behaviour is an emotional issue. Some teachers and students are affected very seriously by the emotional stress that behaviour issues can create. Raising your voice, talking in anger, facing the defiance of a teenager and generally experiencing conflict can be distressing. Some teachers can lose their temper and become extremely angry. Others can become distressed; there can be tears of frustration, anger and even humiliation.

I say this, not to be dramatic, but to acknowledge that this can be a tough business.

If you are going to sustain a long and successful career in teaching, you will need to safeguard your emotional well-being as you meet new classes or move from school to school.

At the same time, you need to take account of your students' emotional well-being. If someone in authority has just shouted at you and given you a public telling off, you don't feel too good about it. If that is accompanied by a sense of injustice, the whole situation can fuel resentment; it's potentially very damaging.

So, for our own sake and for the sake of our students' mental health, we need to acknowledge the emotional levels that individuals operate on in these circumstances. If there has been conflict, if you have lost your temper for any reason or said something in anger that you know will have caused distress, then you should acknowledge it. You should attempt to restore warm, positive relationships as quickly as possible. 'I know I sounded angry; I was getting very frustrated with the behaviour of some individuals.' Give yourself some time to cool down and then move on with a friendly, positive demeanour, breaking the tension that the conflict created.

Just like anything else, behaviour management is easier to master for some than for others. However, it is something that every teacher needs to work at continually. Don't expect it to happen straight away, but work on it; use some of this advice, and it will all come together over time. Remember that there are always plenty of people around to give you support; the hard part is to ask for it, but, once you do, all the problems can be solved.

TALKING POINTS

1   What should you do if you feel that gaining attention from a class for whole-class questioning is proving difficult?
2   What do you do if a small number of students are persistently disruptive and uncooperative?
3   At what point do you use the school systems and impose sanctions, rather than just tell a student off verbally?
4   How do you balance establishing your credibility as an individual teacher with using support from elsewhere to establish the routines and expectations you want for your class?

6 | Classic teaching modes

Great science teaching comprises some well-established 'classic modes'. It is the unique combination of these elements that makes teaching the subject so rewarding.

In this chapter we cover:

- teacher exposition: the power of explaining well;
- whole-class questioning;
- consolidation and practice;
- pair and group work.

The role of practical work and teacher demonstrations follows, in Chapter 7.

Teacher exposition: the power of explaining well

Very often, the simplest and most effective way to get ideas across is to explain them directly to a class, prior to giving the students the opportunity to answer questions or practise problem-solving, based on the concepts in hand. The research by John Hattie (2012) into effective teaching gives this instructional mode a very high rating in terms of effect size. Explaining scientific ideas to a class is, therefore, one of the most important skills to develop for any science teacher.

In this section, we focus on the explanatory input, but throughout consider that the next stage would be for students to have questions or tasks of their own that help them to consolidate their own understanding. In Chapter 8, we'll look at formative feedback in detail, as this too is a critical part of the overall process:

> Teacher explains; students practise; teacher and students exchange feedback; students do more practice. Teacher explains some more . . . and so on.

I've often thought that teachers don't spend enough time rehearsing and sharing their explanations. It should be a central part of our professional dialogue and training. If you are teaching an area of science that is not a particular strength of yours, the most important thing to do is to study it in more depth. I can't stress enough how important this is. Rehearsing your explanations could be part of the process.

There are lots of ways to explain ideas, and, in practising them, you soon find out how well you've understood the science yourself. They include:

1 making ideas as simple and repeatable as possible, gradually increasing the complexity;

2 making connections to everyday life;

3 walking through the ideas with worked examples;

4 using models connecting the abstract to the real;

5 using pictures and diagrams;

6 using analogies.

Let's look at each one in detail.

Making ideas as simple and repeatable as possible, gradually increasing the complexity

In some ways, that sentence is the key to teaching all of science. We always need to make a complex idea simple, to filter out the

Classic teaching modes

excess detail irrelevant to the learners in front of us, while not losing the rigour and depth that they – or least the ablest – are capable of grasping. We also need to show that the same things happen over and over again; science is a story of patterns.

Example: neutralisation reactions

We might start by looking at what the repeated pattern is:

Acid + base → salt + water

On the surface, these reactions involving lots of white powders and clear solutions can be baffling, or they all blur together. We need to give a specific example, using words and symbols to reinforce the connection with a physical demonstration.

Hydrochloric + sodium → sodium + water
acid   hydroxide   chloride

HCl   + NaOH   → NaCl   + H_2O

We might then draw out two parallel ionic reactions:

Making the salt: Na^+ + Cl^- → NaCl

This helps to reinforce the naming protocol, linking the name of salts to the acid. This salt is the salt that we put on our chips or find in the sea. It has an everyday existence we can relate to.

Making the water: H^+ + OH^- → H_2O

This helps to reinforce the idea of neutralisation in terms of pH, which would be covered in practical work or demonstrations. The simplified idea that neutralisation combines hydrogen ions (low pH) and hydroxide ions (high pH) to make neutral water is one you can repeat and reinforce.

Students can then apply the same logic and reasoning to another similar example, say:

Nitric acid and potassium hydroxide: HNO_3 + KOH

You can add complexity by adding another variable, with higher ionic valencies:

Sulphuric acid and copper hydroxide: $H_2SO_4 + Cu(OH)_2$

Here, the equation needs further balancing, and so you need to decide whether that is a point to stress, or whether you are just looking at the naming:

Hydrochloric → chlorides

Nitric → nitrates

Sulphuric → sulphates

Then you can explore ideas presented in reverse by working out which reactants might have produced sodium sulphate, zinc chloride or aluminium sulphate, each requiring more complex balancing. You could also use less familiar reactants, such as ethanoic acid (vinegar).

The idea is to create a ladder of complexity that you move up, as students develop the capacity to move forward.

Making connections to everyday life

As discussed in Chapter 3, scale is an important and often confusing aspect of understanding science. However, if we make connections to what students see and experience, it helps enormously. These ideas illustrate the point:

Following the last section, there are plenty of examples of neutralisation in real life: bee, ant or nettle stings and the traditional neutralising remedies; or indigestion caused by hydrochloric acid in the stomach and the antacid tablets used to treat it. Develop your repertoire of examples and try to learn the chemistry behind them so that you can share it.

Examples of trapped air as a good insulator: chips wrapped in layers of newspaper, take-away coffee cups with crinkled cardboard sleeves, wearing layers of clothes in winter, polar bears with thick fur, double-glazed windows, living in an igloo, sleeping under a duvet. Each example is recognisable – except perhaps the igloo – and shows that the same concept applies in different, real contexts. It is the air that provides the main source of insulation, rather than the materials.

Examples of sound include: the delay between thunder and lightening, the lip-syncing delay at a distance from a big screen, the Doppler effect of a passing car or ambulance siren, the behaviour of musical instruments, the idea of high pitch and low pitch, big amplitude (LOUD) and low amplitude (soft) related to singing or speech. It is unnecessary to teach sound as an abstract idea; there are so many real-life examples to bring into the classroom.

Human senses and reflexes: the range of our hearing, the behaviour of our eyes with near and far objects, how our brains work with numerous optical and sensory effects and illusions, our reaction times, sensations on our skin that indicate heat and pain. Our bodies are living scientific specimens and laboratories, perfect for explaining biological concepts.

Walking through the ideas with worked examples

This applies to any number of problems or questions. For example, when studying kidney function, you could ask students to research the idea themselves and tease out their understanding, but you could simply talk them through it, using visual aids as necessary. This instructional mode is powerful and, even in the most student-centred classrooms, should be routine practice. In other words, just tell them.

> This is how to balance an equation for a chemical reaction: watch and listen.

> This is how to work out the total distance travelled from a velocity–time graph.

> This is how to find the mean of the data from our enzyme experiment.

This might be a model 6-mark answer to 'How does a mammal maintain its body temperature?'.

Spell it out, but keep them with you for each point.

My very strong preference is for students to watch and listen without writing. This ensures that you have their full attention, and that you can check for understanding through questioning as you go along. Pause for a few notes afterwards or ask them to copy down a model answer, if that is what you've set out for them. However, slavish copying or extensive copying of notes can kill the learning, the passion and the focus. It can be deadly.

Once you've modelled the process, students need to practise on their own. So, your exposition needs to be interspersed with periods where students tackle similar questions, rehearsing the techniques that you've shown them, using a range of differentiation strategies as appropriate.

Using models connecting the abstract to the real

As we've discussed earlier, a great deal of scientific understanding is based on models. It is very powerful to make links between what students see with their eyes, what can be visualised in terms of particles and how these can be represented symbolically.

For example, when exploring combustion, you are likely to include the fabulous reaction of burning magnesium. For some students, it is hard to get past the macro experience of a shiny metal turning into a white powder via a very bright glow.

You need a model to explain the chemistry behind it and to explore the bond formation that leads to such a strong energy release.

A particle model for chemical reactions explains several aspects:

- the fact that no atoms are lost, they are just rearranged;
- the balancing of equations, as in Figure 6.1, where it is clear that two atoms of magnesium are needed for each molecule of oxygen. (Ionic bonding is not shown at this stage.)

107

Classic teaching modes

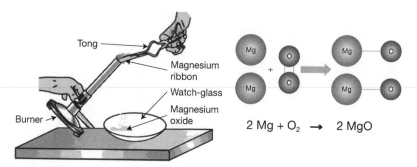

Figure 6.1 Burning magnesium. Linking what we see to conceptual model

Sometimes, an effective model is a highly simplified version of a more complex scenario. In physics, when considering the conservation of momentum, a linear air track is a great piece of kit. You can model a wide range of situations: head-on collisions, explosions, trucks that collide and stick together, elastic and inelastic collisions, jet propulsion. The simplicity of the system, in one dimension, allows some basic calculations to be done that give students a feel for how the theory works.

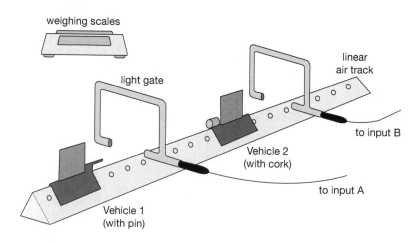

Figure 6.2 The linear air track

A model can also be physical. In explaining digestion, the classic Visking tubing experiment is a superb model of selective absorption through a semi-permeable membrane. In Chapter 7, this is one of the examples of where you need to decide whether a demonstration or class experiment is most appropriate.

Once you get it working, the model is excellent for showing that only the smaller molecules pass through the membrane, leaving the others behind. When an enzyme is added to break down the molecules, it can provide very satisfying evidence to students that the theory actually works in practice.

ACTIVITIES

If you are teaching a topic where a classic model is required, find a time to practise doing the demonstration yourself, making sure you can apply the model to the real situation.

Test out the Visking tubing experiment and make sure you can explain how it models a semi-permeable membrane in the intestines.

Explore all the different linear air track collisions, so you know how to explain how momentum is conserved in head-on collisions, explosions and cases where the riders stick together or 'coalesce'.

Using pictures and diagrams

This may be stating the obvious, but, in science, diagrams are supremely important. This links to the idea of models. It is hard to think of an area of science where diagrams and pictures are not useful. As a science teacher, you are going to become very familiar with these, and it is helpful to learn to draw them well or to seek out excellent examples from elsewhere. Obviously enough, poor

Classic teaching modes

diagrams can be more confusing than anything, so look to make these as high quality as you can.

To illustrate the point, here are some examples.

The phases of the Moon – showing how the Moon appears at different angles around the Earth – can easily be illustrated with some diagrams, perhaps reinforcing a model made with a lamp (Sun) illuminating a tennis ball (Moon) orbiting a football (Earth). It still amazes me how often intelligent people can't explain this phenomenon. No, it is not the Earth's shadow!

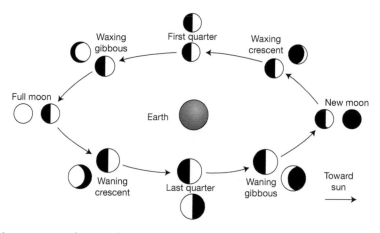

Figure 6.3 Explaining the phases of the Moon

The features of any cell or organ system, or any structural features of a plant or animal, demand a diagram. Here, it is really useful to show photographs alongside a simplified diagram such as Figure 6.4, so that students can make the connections. This also applies to processes such as meiosis and mitosis and fertilisation; the diagram sequence helps tell the story.

Any chemical compound is easier to grapple with if students can make multiple connections. For example, ethane is C_2H_6, represented as $CH_3 - CH_3$, or, visually, as in Figure 6.5a.

Ethene, however, is C_2H_4, represented as $CH_2 = CH_2$, or, visually, as in Figure 6.5b.

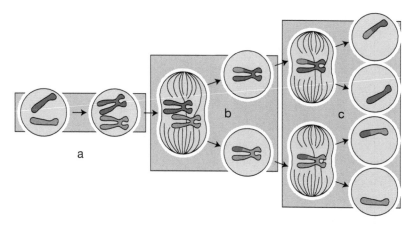

Figure 6.4 A schematic view of meiosis

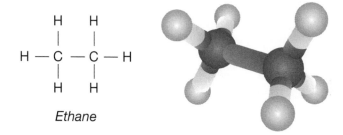

Ethane

Figure 6.5a Ethane molecules seen in two ways

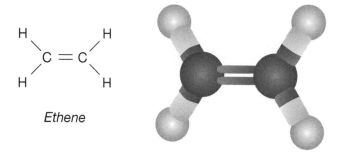

Ethene

Figure 6.5b Ethene molecules seen in two ways

Classic teaching modes

As a general rule, every compound should be shown in all of these forms, to allow students to develop a strong mental model that can underpin the macro-level observations that they make. Name + formula + 2D structure + 3D structure.

When considering the properties of hydrocarbons, for example, there are some very strong patterns linking chain length to viscosity, boiling point and flammability. The visual models are key to constructing a clear mental model that can inform problem-solving and recall.

The features of pieces of equipment, small or large, almost always need to be captured with diagrams, from a standard Bunsen burner set-up to an industrial-scale aluminium smelting plant, from a classroom generator to a nuclear power station, and everything in between. Sometimes, diagrams can become abstract, so, wherever possible, link the diagram to the real object.

A cut-away diagram, showing how the coil in a loudspeaker is orientated relative to the magnetic poles and vibrating cone, makes a lot more sense when positioned alongside a real loudspeaker, with all the parts exposed (Figure 6.6).

Similarly, the standard, simplified heart cross-section makes a lot more sense set beside an actual dissected heart. The muscles, valves and arteries are much more vivid, and, with them side by side, a more complete model is formed (Figure 6.7).

Finally, any mechanics scenario where students need to consider the arrangement of forces, speeds and distances is one where a diagram is needed. It's one of my key physics teaching mantras: *Read the question and draw a diagram.* Every time a student is trying to answer a question but can't visualise the situation, often it is the lack of a diagram that holds them back. If you model this approach yourself, your students are more likely to adopt it.

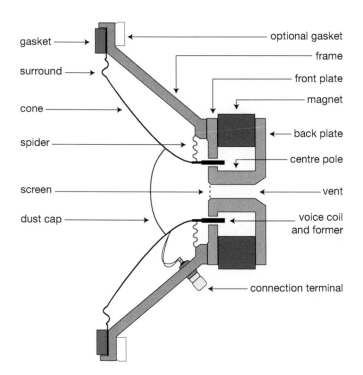

Figure 6.6a A loudspeaker cross-section

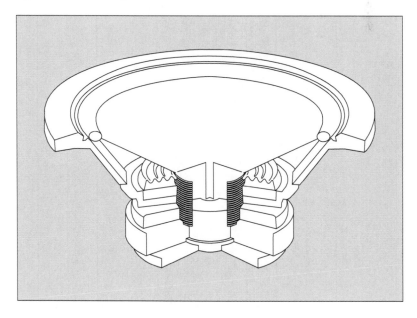

Figure 6.6b The 3D loudspeaker cut-away

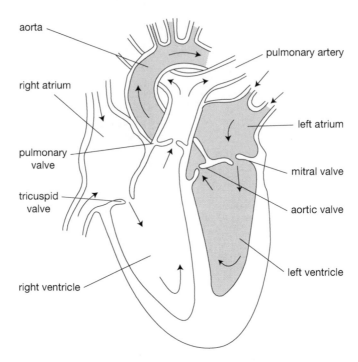

Figure 6.7a A simplified heart cross-section

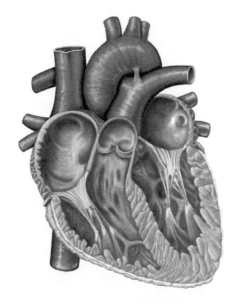

Figure 6.7b A more realistic heart image, closer to real dissection

Source: Stocktrek Images, Inc./Alamy

Using analogies

Analogies are very powerful tools for conveying abstract ideas, both in their capacity to make ideas clearer and in considering the limits of their validity.

Electricity

Developing a deep-level understanding of electricity is one of the most difficult aspects of the science curriculum. The concepts of current, voltage (or potential difference) and resistance, alongside charge, energy and power, are complex and often very confusing. A strong analogy can help to make sense of it all.

The most useful analogy I have found for explaining electricity is to consider the flow of water. There are some good pieces of apparatus that actually show this in action, but it works in abstract too, considering the flow of water from a high reservoir to a lower one, via a range of channels, with a pump to get the water back up again.

- The water is the charge; we could measure the total amount of water that flows.

- The rate of flow of water is the current; at different points, the amount of water flowing per second would vary, but, in a series loop, the value would be the same at every point.

- The pump is the cell or battery, giving energy to the water to return to the high reservoir.

- The difference in height between two parts of the system is the potential difference or voltage: it is the energy lost by each unit of water as it falls down from high ground to low ground.

- The width of each channel would be analogous to the resistance; water could flow faster in a wide channel compared with a thin channel, even if the height dropped was the same.

The properties of series and parallel circuits and various other features of electrical components can be modelled from this analogy. It also helps to make the standard $V = IR$ equation come to life. By asking a number of 'what happens if . . .' questions, you can explore a number of ideas.

My favourite science teacher, Mr Taylor, used to describe the analogy of throwing oranges through a net. Here, the force of the throw was the voltage, the size of the holes determined the resistance, and the number of oranges passing through the net per minute was the current. Why oranges? I have no idea. However, the concept has remained with me for 35 years, and the analogy does work at a basic level.

Solids, liquids and gases

States of matter can be brought alive with the analogy of people joining together in various energy states. This is easily modelled with students in what would certainly be a memorable learning experience if acted out. It can also be done as a thought experiment.

- The solid: students stand in one place, arms forward and sideways to another person's shoulders, with everyone gently swaying, forming a regular structure.

- The liquid: as the students sway more vigorously, it is harder to hold their arms in place, and they break up, now moving around but remaining in close proximity.

- The gas: the students begin to jog around and find that they move further apart with less and less contact.

There are also good kinetic-theory modelling devices in many schools that produce the same effect, vibrating polystyrene balls or marbles at increasing frequency in a glass cylinder. These analogies and models deal with the basic atomic or molecular arrangement, but also hint at the connection between kinetic energy, collisions, intermolecular distances and forces and density – lots of properties can be captured nicely in a model students can see.

Heat transfer

Another excellent use of analogies is when explaining the difference between the types of thermal energy transfer: conduction, radiation and convection. My favourite one is, again, to engage students:

- Conduction: a row of students, sitting side by side, pass tennis balls along the row, vibrating more vigorously as they receive each ball.

- Convection: a selection of students move around in a small area, passing the tennis balls whenever they make contact with each other. If asked to freeze, they can no longer pass the ball – thus modelling the effect of trapping air to prevent convection.

- Radiation: students, at a distance from each other, simply throw the tennis ball from one to the other . . . no medium is needed. Balls can move in all directions, but the 'net flow' is from the high density of tennis balls to the lower density.

Evolution

The concept of the evolutionary tree is so well known that its value as an analogy may actually be lost, unless it is spelled out. Darwin himself used this analogy. The tree's branches and twigs represent diverging species over time, leading to the tips, which represent living species or previous extinctions. The analogy is a very powerful way of demonstrating the concept of 'common ancestors'.

ACTIVITY

For a topic where an analogy will help, such as electricity, take time to rehearse it. What is each element analogous to? What is the current, the voltage and the resistance? Work out where the analogy breaks down and identify any pitfalls that might make the analogy lead to confusion.

Classic teaching modes

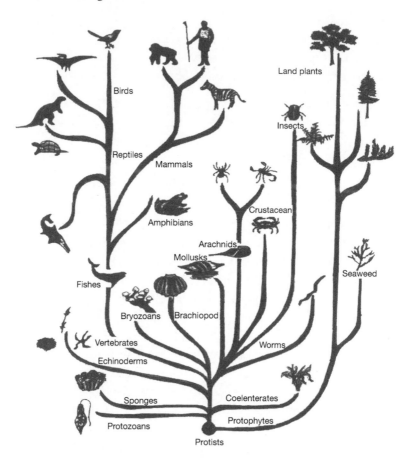

Figure 6.8 The classic Darwinian tree of life analogy

Humans and chimpanzees are different twigs that emerged from a common branch in the past. The same is true of hippos and whales; they are descended from each other, but have common ancestors. Ultimately, all living things have common ancestors with every other living thing, and the tree is a great model for that extraordinary and wonderful fact.

Whole-class questioning

This mode of teaching is likely to dominate your experience as a teacher. Armed with good behaviour management strategies for holding attention and for stop–start discussion, whole-class questioning is a highly productive learning mode that you will use routinely. It simply involves you and your students exchanging questions and answers.

There are a great many variants on this process, but, for the purposes of this chapter, I will focus on four:

- probing
- think–pair–share
- using mini-whiteboards
- dialogic questioning.

In all of these, the goal is to involve as many students as possible in thinking about the concept and developing their understanding, giving as much feedback as possible. You need to ask questions in a way that allows you to identify and challenge misconceptions and allows students to develop an understanding of the how and why of science, not just the what.

For most questions, we want students to know the answer, know why that is the answer and know how to work out the answer.

Probing

In this process, you are essentially conducting a whole-class discussion. In Year 6 my son liked to call them 'conversations', suggesting that it is very much a dialogue among all participants. You ask a series of questions that are designed to seek out the truth in a particular scenario, probing ever deeper.

You need to ensure that the golden rule is strictly adhered to: everyone listens when someone is talking. I would also suggest that this works best with a 'no hands up' rule, so that you are in

Classic teaching modes

complete control of who to bring into the discussion at all times. Students can ask questions by putting hands up, but not plead to answer them.

There is an intensity to this kind of questioning that can be extremely engaging for all concerned: This is an example of the teacher's side of an exchange. The original question concerns the nutrients supplied to a set of plant specimens in different environmental conditions and the projected growth rates.

- Harun, what do you think? Which plant is likely to grow most quickly?

- That's interesting, what makes you think it is Plant D?

- That's true, but what about Plant E. Isn't that the same?

- Sam, is there a different variable we need to consider?

- Can you give an example of what might happen if we increased the CO_2 concentration?

- Can you explain how you worked that out from the graph?

- Sabrina, does that mean we can make plants as big as we like?

- Really? Are you sure? Is there a limiting factor there somewhere?

- Jack, over to you, which of the nutrients makes the biggest impact?

- That's possible. What is the evidence that supports that suggestion?

- Does anyone agree with that? Why?

- OK, Daisy agrees. Does anyone disagree? What would you say instead?

- Right, Clara and Harun. Can they both be correct? How would that be possible?

- But what's the reason for that? Is it just about photo-synthesis or is it something else?

- Fabulous. How did you know that? Where did that idea come from?

- Is that always true or just in this example?

- Minnie. Can you add to that? Is the range of plant sizes directly linked to light? What type of relationship is it?

- I'm not sure if that's quite right . . . have another go . . . is that what you meant?

- That's the gist of it . . . but could you say that more fluently? Let's have that in a full sentence.

Exchanges like this are a key feature of excellent teaching. At a whole-class level, the dialogue is conducted with some energy and passion, moving from student to student, bringing the students from the back and the corners into the fray. There is discipline; everyone listens to everyone else, as the probing continues. Each respondent gets at least one teacher bounce-back, but often repeated exchanges and dialogues develop, as deeper and deeper answers are sought.

ACTIVITY

Probing questioning is a skill you can develop and practise. With a colleague or a sample group of students, take a topic and practise the process of asking ever-deeper questions.

Think–pair–share

This approach to questioning is my default mode. I've written about it in the following article.

THINK–PAIR–SHARE

Every time you ask a question, instead of asking for 'hands up', get the students to think first, then discuss it in pairs before they answer. This simple strategy has transformed how I teach. I've often referred to this as the 'washing hands' of teaching. This is the hospital analogy where the single simplest act, with the greatest impact on patient health, is to ensure every hospital worker washes his or her hands after each patient contact: i.e. changing something that you do all the time, every day, has an enormous impact.

It is worth considering just why 'hands up' is such a poor strategy:

- Only one person gets to answer at a time, so that you have no idea what most people are thinking.
- The answer can be offered before others have had a chance to work it out for themselves.
- Students can opt out of answering or thinking altogether if they choose to. They can hide.
- It is difficult to express confusion or simply to say that you don't know the answer.
- In the 'forest of hands' scenario, the competitiveness inhibits less confident students (and there are gender-specific behaviours here that can't be ignored).
- In the 'blood out of a stone' scenario, you can't tell if students are really stuck or just too unsure of themselves to offer a public answer.
- Very often, 'hands up' goes together with closed questions, with very short think time. We are not comfortable with silence and expect responses within seconds of asking a question.

- Ingrained patterns of behaviour develop: students who always put a hand up, and students who never do.

So, what changes when you ask routinely, 'in your pairs, discuss . . .'?

- Crucially, you are creating a small bubble of security around each pair; a safe space where they can think for a while and say whatever they like. 'I think X', 'No, I think Y' . . . 'I haven't got a clue', 'I wasn't really listening', 'It is more complicated than that . . . maybe it is X except when it is Y?'.
- In this bubble, it is safe to admit you don't understand, and the pair can pluck up the courage together to report this back. It is easier to say 'we don't get it' than 'I don't get it'.
- Every single student can engage in answering the question; they are all generating answers simultaneously – and there is less chance of hiding. Shy students will speak to their partner; the blood comes out of the stone! It has an immediate effect.
- Two heads are better than one. If the question is a good one, pairs can debate their answer. They can then rehearse it and feed back to each other: 'yes, that sounds good but maybe also say this . . .'.
- When the teacher brings the class together to hear answers, the students are repeating something they have rehearsed. It is easy to report back, 'we thought that maybe it is XYZ', when you have already thought this through, compared with being put on the spot with a cold question. It is crucial in the report-back phase to ask selected pairs directly to share their discussion; it means everyone needs to be prepared to report back, in case they are asked. Using a building process is also key here – anything to add, to challenge, any better or different answers? And so on. (It is not always time-efficient to get each pair to share their answer.)

Classic teaching modes

Still now, it is by far the most common piece of feedback I give after lesson observations: If you had asked them to discuss in pairs, the learning would have been better. The question is, why do teachers still ask for hands up, or accept it when students take them down the 'hands up' cul-de-sac? What are the barriers to adopting 'in your pairs' as the default mode of questioning?

- For some, it is about behaviour management. To repeatedly stop and start a class full of kids talking is more difficult than keeping a lid on them and taking one answer at a time. Good stop–start strategies need to be developed and rehearsed.
- It can be overwhelming dealing with all the answers that are generated. After fifteen paired discussions, what do you do then? The key is to encourage active listening and the process of building on previous answers as you sample the responses. Sampling is valid and very much better than only taking a couple of cold hands-up responses.
- Students default to hands up themselves and have to be trained out of it – which can be a drag. This is true, but it soon works if you ignore students with hands up and get the pair discussion going. If you reward 'hands up', that is what you'll get.
- It can feel like a sledgehammer to crack a nut, if you only want to know 'what is the chemical symbol for oxygen' or 'what is 3 × 4'. That is true, but is that a good question in the first place?

This is the crux: think–pair–share forces us to ask better questions. There is room for a few sharp, closed questions in a lesson, but, if we are looking for higher-order thinking, answers that model literacy skills as well as content and, generally, are probing to a deeper level of understanding, then 'hands up', with closed questioning, is never going to be enough.

Once you are into the groove of routine, 'in your pairs' questioning, you find yourself asking better questions – it all flows.

The key to think–pair–share is to ask questions that require thinking and discussion and to use the technique routinely. Even if you don't use the element of pair discussion, take heed of the messages about 'hands up' questioning. It is a fatal error to assume that the class as a whole has understood a concept, simply because one or two keen students have put a hand up and answered correctly.

At the very least, you should insist on selecting students to answer questions and create the expectation that everyone should be prepared to answer at any point, thereby engaging them in listening and thinking. Some teachers like to use randomising methods – using a list of student names in some software or on lolly sticks in a jar – and this can be done well. You need to find your own style.

If you do nothing, your students will almost certainly default to raising hands to answer questions. You should be prepared to change that into something much more effective.

Using mini-whiteboards

I am a big fan of these simple devices. Many schools have them, and, if not, it is very cheap to buy a set of boards, pens and wipers for a class. Mini-whiteboards are very powerful for a variety of reasons:

- The writing is temporary – it will be wiped away – and so students feel less inhibited in attempting to answer.

- Every student answers every question, and you can see all of their answers at once, including wrong answers, partial answers and all the variants on the correct answer.

- Students have a simple means of expressing confusion or doubt that might otherwise remain hidden.

Classic teaching modes

- They can be used to capture diagrams, bullet points, numerical answers and full calculations.

Questions you might ask include the following:

- Show me how the light rays will pass through this convex lens, using a diagram.
- Calculate the area under the velocity–time graph.
- Write out a balanced equation for the thermal decomposition of copper carbonate.
- Draw a sketch diagram of a nephron, showing all the key structures.
- Write out the five key steps in the transpiration of water from a plant's roots to the leaves.
- Explain, in bullet points, what the optimum temperature and pressure for the Haber process are.

Each student uses their board to work out the answer and, then, after a countdown signal, they should all reveal their answers simultaneously. 'Show me.' If they are stuck, they can use a symbol to indicate that. You are then presented with a rich source of feedback about each student's thinking for you to respond to.

- You can select interesting correct answers: 'Why did you express it in that way?'
- You can identify errors and omissions: 'Has everyone got the state symbols on the equation?'
- You can see that perhaps five or ten students really struggled. 'OK, let's go through this again.'
- You can select exemplars to model to the class: 'Look at Sadiq's diagram – he's got it perfectly.'

There is no better way to get this level of immediate response from a class, so I recommend this strategy very highly. Take care not to overuse them – just because the students become weary of them. Also, make sure you keep the phase in the lesson when the boards are out nice and tight. They are not a replacement for notebooks. They are excellent revision aids and great for quick, interactive feedback. Make sure you have a set in your lab.

Dialogic questioning

The final questioning strategy I'd like to highlight is an approach that works very well whenever you have a good complex question and a class of students who can concentrate and listen for a more extended period.

The idea is that you select one student, either spontaneously or by preparing them in advance, and direct a series of questions at them for several minutes, while other students listen. In doing this, you engage in a dialogue that allows you to probe more deeply into a question than you might be able to if you scan from student to student, spreading the questions around the class.

The flow of questions may follow a pattern similar to the probing questions above, but, because the same student is responding, they are drawing on their knowledge and understanding in a very focused way, guided by you to make the connections.

Importantly, although this has a huge benefit for the person in the hot seat, it is also useful for everyone else, provided that they are encouraged to listen and are expected to use the ideas themselves in subsequent work.

You might, for example, ask a student to prepare to discuss the analysis of an experiment. You then engage them in a dialogue about their results, the errors, the relationships, the conclusions, the link to the theory, improvements to the method that would result in a more accurate set of data. Other members of the class listen as a detailed, focused set of answers is aired, modelling the process of analysing results for them to mirror in their own work.

Consolidation and practice

An important element of the learning process is to convert all the inputs from your explanations, students' practical learning, class discussions and observations into stored knowledge and understanding that can be recalled and applied in a range of contexts. This might be straightforward factual knowledge, or a range of analytical skills.

In any series of lessons, you need to provide students with ample opportunities to process and store their learning. This is the gritty side of things, the hard graft, the focused practice and consolidation that all learners need. It could be a phase in a multitask lesson or it could be that you devote entire lessons to this kind of activity, in a flow of lessons where the activities are more varied over time.

As well as using lessons, you also have scope to direct students to engage in these activities as part of their homework or self-study. How you divide up the time is part of the planning process, and, as ever, a healthy variety is a sensible approach.

There are broadly two types of work in this area:

Problem-solving

A cornerstone of learning in science is the process of answering questions, solving problems and analysing data. Depending on your school context and the topic in hand, you are likely to have a range of resources at your disposal, from worksheets, textbooks, photocopied exam questions, to websites or software applications, which will provide you with an array of possibilities.

You can, of course, devise your own questions to produce your own worksheets, or simply write them on the board. The key thing is to plan these questions in advance, with suitable differentiation built in and enough scope to adjust if students' responses suggest that the questions are too easy or too difficult, or have been covered sufficiently to move on.

Take time to get to know your textbooks. Many are excellent at providing a comprehensive set of questions linked to good explanatory information. However, they are not always as good or consistent as you might like. Sometimes, the questions are too easy or too difficult; sometimes, they don't cover the material in the exact way that you have approached it, so some knowledge might be assumed that you haven't covered yet.

You may find that the text in the books gives away the answers too cheaply for many students, such that they don't really have to know much beyond recognising key words.

For example, if the text says, 'Pasta and bread are good sources of carbohydrates', it doesn't take them very far if the question on the page is: 'Suggest a good source of carbohydrates'. Students can answer this without knowing anything about food at all. (Try this: 'Rooba and Stip are two types of Fagga. Name two types of Fagga.') All this does is encourage students to scan a text for the words, without engaging with their meaning. Take care to ensure these questions are avoided or do not dominate.

It pays to use a variety of sources for questions. This is partly because it can become very dull and repetitive if the routine is textbook, questions, textbook, questions. Similarly, the 'death by worksheet' cliché is firmly rooted in students' negative experience. However, the need for variety is mainly because different sources tend to frame questions in different styles, and this increases students' capacity to think and to apply their knowledge in different contexts.

Exercise books and worksheets

On a very practical level, it is very helpful to establish rules and routines for students managing their work. This might be a departmental policy, or something left to you to decide. Consider things such as:

- dates and titles;
- underlining;

Classic teaching modes

- using pen for writing and pencil for diagrams;
- insisting on straight lines drawn with rulers;
- starting every new topic on a new page, or use every page fully;
- writing answers in full sentences;
- making reference to page numbers for textbook questions;
- sticking worksheets and graph paper in with glue, or using some other storage method;
- always stating equations before substituting the numbers for calculations.

The list could go on. The point is to make sure you are clear about what you expect, and that you communicate this to your students, reinforcing your expectations as necessary.

Exam questions

When you have examination classes, a key element in your students' success will be the level of familiarity with the style of questions in the exams and their confidence in formulating answers of the required standard. Exam questions are usually divided into multiple elements that range from simple, one-word responses up to extended, 4–8-mark answers, including a wide range of calculation- or data-based questions. As we will see in Chapter 8, formative assessment based on students' responses to their practice questions is really the main route to success, and so they need as much of this type of practice as you can give them.

It is extremely important to know the style of exam questions for any syllabus that you teach, in advance of teaching the topic. Take time to look through past papers that your school has, or look on the exam board websites for their exemplars and archives. There are also good packages such as ExamPro that allow teachers to compile tailored sets of questions from a large database, searching by topic and level of difficulty. You can then generate the accompanying mark scheme for your marking or for using in peer- and self-assessment.

Knowing the style of questions will influence all of your question–answer exchanges with students and will help to focus their learning, so that the exam preparation process feels like a natural extension of their regular lessons. Your knowledge might include which equations and reactions need to be known from memory, and which will be provided on a formula sheet; how numerical questions should be set out; and the protocols for units and symbols. It will also include knowing which topic areas are likely to feature in more extended answers.

ACTIVITIES

Use a range of resources to compile a set of excellent differentiated questions to make a worksheet that gets more difficult as you go through it. Try to write some of your own questions and add these to the worksheet. This will help you to consider how questions can be designed to provide evidence of learning.

Evaluate the effectiveness of the worksheet once your students have done the work. Did it provide challenge for all students? Did it help you to know how well they'd learned the topic?

Recording and reporting

Aside from problem-solving, there is a lot of very valuable work to be done that can be generated by students themselves, where they take ideas from various sources to create a product of some kind that illustrates their understanding. These tasks can be rather low-level activities, transferring information from one place to another and organising it in some form. They can also be more challenging, requiring students to select, compare, analyse and explain the ideas as part of the process.

Classic teaching modes

Be wary of the possibility for 'find out' research tasks or 'make a poster' activities to generate responses that do not secure scientific learning. Students can copy swathes of text and images from the Internet, or create elaborate, artistic, visual products that have almost no scientific content – unless you anticipate this and direct them towards a more rigorous outcome. As we see in Chapter 8, the use of clear success criteria is the way to do this.

Forms of response that can be highly valuable might include the following:

Research notes

It is really helpful to teach students to extract the salient points from a text or website to make their own notes. This liberates lesson time for discussion and practical work and can provide students with their own reference material to aid recall. The idea of writing 'in your own words' needs to be developed, although this can be difficult to do in some circumstances.

If you establish a routine for note making, students can get into the rhythm of it: state the key concept; include an illustrative diagram; record equations and definitions of new terms; and give an example of the phenomenon in action. Some students may well benefit from using a note-making writing frame such as a 'fact file' template, whereas others will be able to work independently.

Report documents

There is room in science for essay writing, although it is not common. It might be something you set as a task occasionally. It is more likely that you will ask students to produce explanatory reports in answer to some specific scientific question, or to present information for a particular purpose:

- Produce a scientific report outlining the key issues surrounding genetically modified crops, with a conclusion of your own. Imagine this is to be published in a scientific journal for sixth form students.

- Find out about a rare plant or animal. Describe its features and explain how it has evolved to be well adapted to its natural habitat.

- Explain how plastics are produced from crude-oil products, using diagrams as appropriate and giving examples of some specific cases.

- Produce a leaflet for young people outlining the dangers of obesity/smoking/alcohol, including the key biological information.

- Write a dialogue between two people with opposing views regarding the value of fracking as a means of securing natural gas from the Earth's crust. Focus on the scientific detail, as well as any social implications.

In order to complete these tasks, students may benefit from having access to a library or the Internet, in addition to the standard textbooks. You should bear that in mind if setting this kind of task for homework, establishing how each student will manage the task if they don't have access to these things at home. Although the examples given suggest some focus and structure, in practice, many students would need much more specific guidance, and, again, the use of success criteria would secure much better outcomes.

Multimedia products

In addition to standard writing tasks, there are numerous other ways in which students can create products that communicate their understanding. Again, it is important to make sure that the content is rigorous, and that the 'fun factor' doesn't override the scientific learning.

Just because students are busy and engaged, it does not mean that they are learning. Structure these tasks so that new learning is built in and so that, in order to meet the success criteria, students have to demonstrate strong understanding of the science and not just good 'copy and paste' skills.

Classic teaching modes

Here are some examples:

- Websites and blogs: Create a web page that pulls together images, video and text in your own words, explaining the story behind the Large Hadron Collider at CERN, Geneva. You may need to show students how to do this, but, if left as an option, you may find that several students know how to set up a blog already. Whenever possible, ask students to show each other how to do the technical work.

- Storyboards: Use pictorial sequences to tell the story of sexual reproduction in plants, or the rock cycle. This could be hand drawn or created using a computer.

- Videos: Make a video about an 'eco house', outlining all the features that enable the owner to save energy. This is increasingly easy to do for students with mobile phones and a laptop. A video can combine audio presentation with images to explain concepts in depth. These can then be shared with the class. Students should be encouraged to plan their script in advance and to pay attention to the sound quality, as the audio is technically often the weak area in the production process.

- iPads: Use the app 'Explain everything' or something similar to show how hard water can be softened, including images and all the appropriate chemical equations.

- Make a Powerpoint or Prezi presentation aimed at students your age, showing them how a crumple zone and other features in a car protect passengers in the event of an accident, making reference to the concept of momentum. Writing a script for an auto-play presentation with a voice over is another variation.

Open-ended response format

My favourite strategy for this kind of work is to combine the classwork with homework, leaving the format completely open for students to choose. In terms of securing the scientific under-standing, it does not matter particularly whether a student makes a video, writes a report or produces a leaflet.

By giving them a choice, you end up with a good variety of products to share in the class, and students develop the confidence to make decisions about their learning, rather than always feeling it is a question of doing only what the teacher says.

Pair and group work

In many respects, pair and group work do not really constitute a different learning mode as such; they are simply ways of organising the class. You are likely to ask students to work in pairs and groups routinely to do most of their practical work, to discuss questions and to engage in projects such as making videos. This will be in order to share equipment and to facilitate differentiation.

However, in all of these cases, you need to be clear about the reason for using the method, rather than asking students to work by themselves. Effective group work needs to structured and rehearsed, so that the learning of all the individuals is enhanced by the process, rather than restricted.

In other words, don't do group work for the sake of it; if you feel students would learn better working alone in a particular situation, then they should.

The key features of successful group work are as follows:

- Every student has a clear role, such that they must contribute.

- No student can dominate unduly, even though some might have leadership roles.

- No student can opt out, masking passive behaviour with the endeavours of the other members of their group.

- The learning outcomes are enhanced through the collaborative process.

In practice, it is very hard to be certain of the last point, but it is worth bearing in mind when evaluating outcomes. It is essential to make the dynamics of effective group work an explicit issue with students. If they understand the rationale for the group structure, they are more likely to buy in to the various strategies you might use.

Here are some effective group work strategies.

Firstly, create the expectation that any individual may be required to report back to the class. This might involve asking each group member to be numbered, say 1–4, and then selecting a number (or using a random selection tool) when choosing who will give the report. It works extremely well, especially if you make this a routine practice.

In anticipation of the possibility that they might be asked to represent the group, every student must engage fully with what is going on; the more able or more dominant group members need to ensure that their peers have a good chance to represent the group well. This leads to great discussions and peer-to-peer teaching.

A second strategy is to give each group member an assigned role. You can establish set roles for a group task that students allocate themselves or that are allocated by you. This might be equivalent to chair, scribe and reporter. It might be a division of labour in relation to a research task, where students need to focus on a specific area and then share their findings with their group.

For example, each Year 8 student needs to produce a summary of the way a particular food group is broken down during digestion to inform a group presentation.

It might be related to a specific class practical: someone to measure the time, someone to release the reactants and someone to mix up the concentrations in advance.

My very strong preference is that every student should record results and observations during practical work, rather than asking them to copy from a recorder later. Slavish copying of sets of results is very time consuming and, very often, it leads to problems. 'What do we do Miss? Hamish wrote down the results last lesson and he's not in today?' This happens far too often, so avoid it if you possibly can.

Until you have your class trained to do these things automatically, take time to spell out your expectations; otherwise, you will have some students standing around watching, while the others do all the work and all the thinking. This might be laziness on their part, or simply a lack of assertiveness in the face of others' über-enthusiasm.

A third strategy is to set collective goals for the group that are based on every student participating and making progress with their learning. The most obvious goal would be that everyone helps everyone in the group to complete a task; for example, they all have a completed table of results and a graph.

You can also use group structures to solve problems. You could give out a set of questions that students must all answer correctly within a time limit, with different members of the group holding one of the model answers. They need to give appropriate feedback to their peers sufficiently well that everyone has a full set of correct answers.

When combined with the first strategy, this is a powerful technique as part of a variety of practice activities. Depending on the class dynamics, it can be very effective to make this a competition between all the groups in the class. Very often, the motivating effect of group competitions is very high. They have to decide whether to rush and risk making errors, or take their time to get the problems right.

Presentations and debates are both excellent examples of group work that can be used to good effect, although there are pitfalls that you need to avoid. In Chapter 8, there is a section on suggested success criteria for good presentations, and the idea that students should have the opportunity to improve them, both in terms of content and delivery.

The important thing here is to be sure that every student contributes more or less equally, and that the process of giving a presentation or conducting a debate enhances their learning of the science, as well as providing an opportunity to develop their confidence with public speaking.

Classic teaching modes

In both cases, the process should give you an opportunity to pick up on misconceptions, especially if the class as a whole has a role alongside you as teacher in asking questions, challenging the speakers and presenters. It should not be a case of passive listening, followed by a lame 'well done', before the next group steps up.

Presentations should allow new ideas and strong explanations to be shared. Debates should allow genuine discussion about scientific ideas and their social and ethical consequences to be aired. It is great fun to use formal debating structures, although that is not always necessary or time efficient.

Topics that might be the subject of presentations or debates include:

- the use of stem cells in research for cancer treatments;

- the development of artificial meat grown in laboratories;

- investing public money in wind power, instead of building nuclear power stations;

- the value to society of space exploration;

- the use of pesticides in agriculture in developed and developing countries;

- the extent to which carbon emissions can and should be controlled to reduce climate change;

- the issues surrounding establishing a new hydroelectric dam;

- the issues surrounding the culling of badgers to prevent the spread of TB to cattle.

It is worth stressing that students must have sufficient knowledge of a topic in order to engage in a debate. Ill-informed debates can simply reinforce misconceptions or over-simplified scientific ideas gleaned from poorly evidenced newspaper articles.

As we discussed in Chapter 2, some ideas in science are no longer debatable, and you should tackle students who regurgitate tabloid myths that have no scientific basis. It is one of the most important jobs for science teachers to do.

ACTIVITY

For a topic you are going to teach, plan where you could employ group work, such as a presentation, or where you could include a formal debate.

TALKING POINTS

1   Which of the classic teaching modes are you most or least likely to use? Will this depend on the topic, or is it a matter of your own confidence?
2   For any given concept, how well can you explain it? What is the appropriate depth of explanation required for the students you teach to excel?
3   How can you engage all of your students in the process of answering questions, when they have different levels of understanding and different levels of confidence in offering answers?

7 Science as a practical subject

In this chapter, we will celebrate the aspect of science that is often the greatest source of joy for many students and teachers. We'll tackle a range of issues associated with experimental work in a typical school laboratory classroom and explore the role of practical science in supporting students' conceptual understanding.

There are two main aspects to practical work that we will look at in detail:

- demonstrations: the classic 'front-bench demo';
- class practicals: experiments and investigations.

However, before you get involved in planning any practical work, you need to have a good understanding of three areas:

- the role of technicians;
- the importance of health and safety in the laboratory;
- the range of equipment, materials and apparatus at your disposal.

Working with technicians

In almost every situation where you're likely to teach, there will be science technicians employed as part of the team. The ratio of technicians to teachers varies enormously, and each team will have its own blend of subject specialist knowledge and experience.

You may work with someone with years of experience in school science, prior experience of teaching or working in industry and high-level academic and professional qualifications in one or more science areas. Alternatively, you may be working with someone who is learning the role alongside you, who may be more of a general technician and have less of an academic background.

Whatever the circumstances, it is vital that you establish a good working relationship with the technicians who will support your lessons from the very beginning. Usually, it is a case of exchanging ideas, so that you and the technicians benefit from each other's knowledge and experience.

As far as possible, you should involve technicians in every aspect of your planning:

- Make sure they know the overarching plan for the year and for each unit of work, and seek their input wherever possible.

- Learn about the range of resources that are available, so that you can select the materials and equipment you need. This has a major bearing on how you plan to teach. It is important to be familiar with all the equipment and resources you will use in a lesson in advance, and technicians can help you with this.

- Plan specific lessons in detail, right down to the numbers of stop-clocks and test tubes and the amounts of any consumable solutions and other materials.

- Consider the risk assessments for your lessons and any planning that follows to ensure that all the safety risks are mitigated in an appropriate manner.

An important rule you should stick to is this: **Never undertake a demonstration or class experiment with equipment you have not used before.**

At the level of short-term lesson planning, most schools operate a straightforward requisitions system, whereby teachers write down what they need for each lesson in advance, and technicians then put the resources and equipment together at the allotted time.

Science as a practical subject

Clear communication and a shared understanding of any shorthand codes are vital.

My main advice about requisitions is to make sure you stick to the deadline set by the team. Often this would be, say, Thursday lunchtime for the whole of the following week. Sometimes, schools operate a rolling three-day warning system. Of course, there will be times when you need to make changes; you must be prepared to adjust your planning in response to your students' progress and any number of unforeseen circumstances.

If you are usually punctual with your requisitions, the technicians will be sympathetic when you need to make last-minute requests for additional items, or if you forget something and need drastic help. This also works both ways. Sometimes, technicians do not provide the equipment that you think you've asked for. This could be because you didn't make it explicit enough, or because of an error or difficulty at their end.

It pays to be flexible and understanding in both directions, although, ultimately, you are the person with the responsibility for delivering excellent lessons. You need to be the person who sets the standards, ensuring that the resources and equipment that you need for the specific area of learning are there when you and your students need them.

Your technician team will have certain expectations around their capacity to participate in the lessons, working with students, or to set equipment up in advance. For example, you may need a ripple tank set up for a demonstration, or a set of water baths set up and preheated, in order to conduct work on rates of reactions within the limits of an hour-long lesson.

This is an important area to establish in advance. Don't assume the equipment will be set up for you, unless this is something you have discussed or communicated clearly.

It is a good habit to get into to evaluate your lessons with the technicians who have supported you. If you feel that some adjustments are needed – for example, if different-strength acids or enzyme concentrations would be better – then you need to give this feedback to the technicians for the next lesson or for future reference.

Health and safety

There are a lot of myths around this area of science teaching, suggesting that virtually all of the 'fun stuff' has been banned for being too dangerous. This is simply untrue. Aside from the foolhardiness of associating 'fun' with 'danger', there are very many experiments and demonstrations that you can do in school laboratories that are immensely engaging, and plenty that involve significant danger. Good school science is conducted in a culture that is 'risk aware' but not 'risk averse'. There is an important distinction.

It would be impossible for me to provide a comprehensive guide to every aspect of health and safety in a book like this. However, you should take time to learn as much as you can, focusing on the details as and when you need them. For most experiments, you will need to be sure that a relevant risk assessment has been completed.

Very often, these are done centrally, on behalf of the whole department. For example, most schools will use the Hazcard system run by CLEAPSS. This is an organisation dedicated to this activity. Hazcards are A5 cards containing the key safety measures that should be in place for a very wide range of standard school practicals and demonstrations.

They include the precautions that should be taken and recommend actions that should be taken if anything goes wrong. You should read them in advance and make sure you know where all the safety equipment is: fire blankets, fire extinguishers, eye baths, first aid kit, and so on.

Other good sources of information include the website of the Association of Science Educators (**www.ase.org.uk**) and the knowledge and experience of your teaching colleagues and technicians, who will normally undertake specialist training covering the latest guidelines.

Science as a practical subject

Some common areas that you will need to know about are set out below. Please note that this is absolutely not a comprehensive list. It is just a small selection, chosen to illustrate the general issue.

Activity	Health and safety considerations
General laboratory activities	You'll need a clear set of general classroom rules that cover walking and not running, avoiding trip hazards, awareness of spillages, appropriate use of sinks and electrical sockets and adherence to the stop safety command
Using Bunsen burners and tripods	Burns are a serious risk and constitute a high proportion of laboratory injuries. Eyes, eyebrows, hair and hands are vulnerable. Safety glasses or goggles are essential. Allow a cool-off period before transporting hot tripods by the feet and carrying beakers. Take care with heating materials of any kind; metals, wax and oil can become extremely hot without it being immediately obvious
Concentrated solutions: acids and alkalis	Eye-splash injuries are the biggest concern, alongside skin burns. Disposable gloves, safety glasses and careful handling are the key elements
Explosive reactions	Safety screens and ear protection can be needed. Sometimes, it is necessary to go outside, e.g. for a big hydrogen–oxygen mix explosion. Potassium on water needs a safety screen, because of erratic movement of the floating metal and final fizzing pop
Handling chemicals and glassware	In general, there is a risk of burns and cuts. Smashed glass and chemical spills are relatively common occurrences, so well-known procedures to clear these up are needed. There are also risks of swallowing (students might lick a stirring rod absentmindedly!) and breathing in acidic or toxic fumes. Some chemicals should only be produced by a teacher and/or only in a fume cupboard

Activity	Health and safety considerations
Animal dissections and tissue samples	Different organs and tissues have specific requirements. Using gloves and safety glasses is common. Fainting at the sight of a heart or lung (from a sheep) is common, and falling injuries can result
Live microbes	There are strict rules about handling bacteria of different strains. Follow the procedures very closely. Some are more freely used, as with yeast in breadmaking and fermentation
High-voltage electricity	A Van der Graaf generator or EHT (high-voltage) supply can produce several kilovolts. These need to be handled carefully to ensure that high resistances are present
Using radioactive sources	Strict rules govern the use of these sources, including their storage and safe handling. Students need to be over 16 to handle sources. A log needs to be kept registering the exposure time for the person handling each source
Using electrical equipment in general	Any piece of equipment can overheat or experience a short circuit. General awareness of electrical safety is needed, and avoidance of excessively high currents, which can cause a fire risk and possible shocks

ACTIVITY

Arrange a session with one of your technicians to go through the safety issues for the topics you are going to teach in the near future. Familiarise yourself with the formal safety guidelines and discuss them with colleagues, so that you keep them in proper perspective, making sure you are not too cautious, limiting students' experience.

Teaching laboratory safety

It is likely to be a feature of the curriculum early on in your students' secondary-school lives. In truth, health and safety is unlikely to be anyone's favourite topic if it is merely a paper exercise, where most of the potential hazards seem remote and hypothetical.

The trick is to deal with the safety issues pertinent to a given practical situation and to build them into your routines. For example, it may be standard practice for students to wear aprons or lab coats, along with safety glasses, when conducting chemistry experiments.

It is down to you to model a common-sense approach that achieves an appropriate level of risk awareness, without becoming obsessively overcautious. Never appear cavalier or gung-ho about serious safety matters, but, at the same time, make sure that you don't kill the joy of experimental work by being overly anxious. If things go wrong, try to model the calm, pragmatic response you expect from your students.

Whenever it is relevant, use science topics to learn about safety. For example, electrical safety is part and parcel of learning about voltage and current, fuses and earth wires. Safety with chemicals can be reinforced when learning about neutralisation reactions, hydrocarbons or the reactivity series with metals. The health risks from microbes are automatically reinforced when they are handled in a highly safe manner.

Apparatus, equipment and materials

It would be foolish to try to draw up a comprehensive list of science equipment that you might encounter. However, it is worth exploring what you have at an early stage in any school, as this will influence your schemes of work. There is a lot of standard equipment, but every school I have worked in has had several unique pieces of equipment that threw up various possibilities.

Whether you have a specific science background or a very general one, there will always be some pieces of equipment and some materials that you have never handled before. As you work through each topic for the first time, you need to devote time to becoming familiar with the basic operation of the equipment and try to work out some of the nuances.

You will not do yourself or your students any favours if you simply busk through a lesson, fiddling about with kit as a complete novice. You can't take a short cut to real experience, but you can give yourself a head start by finding out as much as you can before you're using the apparatus in front of students.

It is worth restating the golden rule: **Never undertake a demonstration or class experiment with equipment you have not used before**. This is doubly true if there are any major health and safety considerations.

ACTIVITY

Some of the resources and equipment you may need to become familiar with are shown in the list on the following pages. Look at the equipment you are less familiar with and, taking heed of the considerations noted, practise setting up the experiments and demonstrations in advance of your lessons.

Please note that the following list is only intended to be illustrative, as there is so much more, but I've tried to include some of the items most likely to need your attention.

EQUIPMENT/RESOURCES AND THINGS TO CONSIDER

- **Standard lab equipment: beakers, Bunsen burners, retort stands**
  You should know how to assemble a standard Bunsen burner set-up and where to locate the equipment that is stored in your lab, accessible without the need for a specific requisition

- **Electrical circuits: meters, power packs, components, leads**
  Make sure the ammeters and voltmeters can measure the current and voltage ranges for the experiments you do. Learn to use the shunts, multipliers and the multimeters available to you, so students can take readings. Do you need 12 V power packs, or will lower voltage cells be sufficient? Practise trouble-shooting circuits; it is often a case of bad connections in the leads, but meters and components do fail from time to time. Report these issues to the technicians

- **Basic measurement equipment**
  Know where to locate stop-clocks, thermometers, measuring cylinders, volumetric glassware, metre rulers and balances. Identify any idiosyncratic functions in all basic equipment

- **Plants and related items**
  Technicians will need to obtain the specimens so they are fresh enough for your lessons. Photosynthesis experiments may depend on freshly de-starched leaves, which requires plants to be prepared in advance. Anticipate variable success with seed germination and plant growth, making sure you have plenty of specimens included to increase the odds of success

- **Animal organs**
Again, these are obtained in a tight time frame; defrosted organs are rarely as good as fresh ones. A heart–lung pluck is great fun, but they often have flaws when pumped with air. Test them in advance, on arrival. Try out an eye or kidney dissection if you have never done one before. Rat or frog dissections are complex; practise or ask to watch an experienced person show you how to do it. Take note of some students' ethical objections and fainting potential

- **Microscopes**
These are often very fiddly, and it helps to know how the specific models in your school work. Practise with pre-made slides and ones you make yourself. A lot of time can be wasted forming an image rather than studying a specimen, unless you can intervene in a knowledgeable manner. Always start at low magnification and move in closer, once your specimen is in range

- **Electronics kits**
There are lots of models on the market, of varying complexity. Many incorporate op amps, microchips or transistors that may not be part of the syllabus. Bear this in mind, using equipment that supports the learning rather than over-complicates it. It really pays to play around with them yourself

- **Oscilloscopes**
A good-quality dual-beam oscilloscope can be baffling to the uninitiated. Make sure you can obtain a trace from a signal generator at different frequencies and voltage outputs, troubleshooting with the grounding function and the zero adjustments

  Trigger levels are often fiddly on intermittent or low-voltage inputs

Science as a practical subject

- **Van der Graaf generator**
  Atmospheric conditions play a significant role in how well these work. A good rub with emery paper can remove oxide layers that reduce the electrostatic effects. Test in advance, taking care to discharge the dome to earth rather than through your hands. Explore the attachments, tin-foil cups, cotton or string, and rehearse the classic 'hair on end' demo

- **Geiger–Müller tube and radioactive sources**
  Alongside the health and safety issues, familiarise yourself with the activity of your sources. Make sure you can handle the sources correctly as part of an absorption thickness or inverse-square source–detector distance experiment

- **Chemicals and mineral resources**
  Well-selected concentrations and quantities of materials determine the success of many experiments in all three sciences. Work with technicians to get the right ranges of acid or enzyme concentrations to generate reaction rates within a range that allows multiple tests in one lesson. Test or seek advice on appropriate quantities of any substance students might use in their experiments. For any quantity that students need to vary – length of wire, volume of indicator, mass of compounds or metals, temperature range, time intervals for best results – it really helps to know roughly what the optimum range should be. Students may be asked to work this out themselves, but you should be able to guide them, spotting obvious poor choices or mistakes

- **Burettes and titrations**
  Titration techniques require practice both to ensure accurate measurement and to reduce contamination during multiple measurements. The basic set-up and methodology, as well as the handling of fragile glassware, are worth rehearsing

- **Fractional distillation apparatus**
  If you can set up and operate a standard classroom fractional distillation demonstration, you'll have practised several skills that could be useful elsewhere. These include using a condensing tube, extracting different fractions for subsequent testing and heating a liquid to high temperature with bumping granules. The original mixture is the key to success; it can be engineered to give good results for demonstration purposes

- **Fume cupboard**
  Some reactions must be conducted in the fume cupboard because of the toxic fumes, producing hydrogen sulphide or hydrogen chloride, for example. They have gas taps and water supplies to negotiate, as well as extraction features

- **Data-logging equipment**
  A wide range of data-loggers exist in schools. They can be designed to measure almost any variable and might be connected to a laptop or have built-in displays. They provide superb additions to other measurement devices, and it pays to become confident setting up the equipment, even if you receive good technician support. Often, there are subtle issues with calibration or configuring axes on the software. Various other import/export issues can also present difficulties, unless you know what to do

- **Standard chemical and biological tests**
  You may be teaching students to test for starch and for glucose using iodine and spotting tiles or Benedict's solution. You might be using a range of chemical tests, such as solubility or flame tests. Being familiar with the nuances of these tests, knowing what a positive or negative result looks like in practice, will help you enormously

Practical work and conceptual understanding

Before you engage in any practical work, you need to think about the reasons for doing it. You should also consider the sequence of the practical components relative to other parts of the learning process.

- Is the main aim to use the practical experience to develop some conceptual understanding in a particular topic?
- Is the main aim to develop a generic or specific skill in conducting experiments?
- Should the theory precede the practical work, or should the practical work provide a means of approaching the theory?

You should then look at the pragmatic considerations:

- How much time have we got for this?
- How much equipment do we have? Is there enough for a class set, or is this definitely a one-off piece of apparatus.
- How complex is the practical set-up in relation to the learning points in hand?
- How many, and what range of, values of a given variable can realistically be measured in the circumstances we're in?

Taking all this into account, you can then make the key decisions:

- Do you organise a teacher demonstration?
- Do you engage students in a class experiment?
- Do you set up a more open-ended practical investigation?

Or, do you simply tackle the topic theoretically, possibly referencing some video material or other resources to bring the ideas off the page. There are lots of online simulations, for example, where you can change a number of variables to explore what effect that has.

In reality, you are likely to mix demonstrations and class practicals across a flow of lessons. In many cases, your decision is easy, because of the availability of equipment and resources or the safety implications.

Classic teacher demonstrations might include:

- a sheep's lung: inflating the lung with a foot pump to replicate breathing, making connections from the organ to the bronchioles and alveoli they can't see;

- electrolysis of ionised water in the Hoffmann process: collecting and testing the gases formed at each electrode;

- demonstration of a power-line system, showing how much energy is lost without using step-up and step-down transformers at each end;

- the workings of a ripple tank, using a strobe light to capture a range of wave phenomena;

- the reactions of Group I metals with water, behind a safety screen;

- a 'smoking machine' showing the content of inhaled smoke from cigarettes as it passes through cotton wool and universal indicator;

- the reaction of concentrated sulphuric acid with sucrose, releasing an awe-inspiring column of carbon and lots of heat energy;

- the kicking wire experiment, showing the force exerted on current-carrying wires in magnetic fields, then linking this to electric motors;

- methane bubble combustion: trapping gas under detergent to make bubbles and igniting them to show energy release; links to flammability of hydrocarbons, e.g. pentane and hexane;

- testing the range of human hearing using a signal generator and speaker;

Science as a practical subject

- comparing the skeletal features of a range of real specimens;

- the conductivity of lead chloride in solid form and molten form, illustrating the properties of an ionic structure and the concept of current being a movement of charged particles.

In each case, specialist equipment or safety requirements will suggest that these are demonstrations. However, it can also be because you want to focus on the learning in a specific way.

ACTIVITY

Explore these demonstrations and any others that you know you need to give. Practise them and rehearse how you will link the demonstration to the learning aims of a lesson and the explanations you want to give. What questions could you ask during the demonstration to elicit responses that require an appropriate depth of understanding?

In the detailed examples below, there is a more complex decision to make.

Example: Learning about enzymes

It helps students to understand enzyme function and the fact that the reactions occur over a measurable time period to see and experience the standard starch test being done. Using a spotting tile to test samples with iodine when reacting amylase with starch can be illuminating; eventually, the iodine stops changing colour, because the starch has all been broken down.

It is part of the learning for students to understand this method; it is, therefore, a good idea for them to do this as a class experiment. There is usually plenty of equipment, and it is easy to set up at room temperature.

It is also part of the learning in science for students to know about repeatability and accuracy: can they get the same result twice? Again, this experiment provides the opportunity to explore some generic ideas about measurement in a biological context – which is much more difficult than in physics.

However, the next stage is to vary the temperature, to show the impact this has on the rate of reaction. The main aim is to learn that there is an optimal temperature for the reaction.

Now, setting up a series of controlled temperature environments is essentially a logistical task. It has nothing to do with enzymes.

With younger or less able students, it can be very difficult to get a decent set of results for everyone, with accurate data ranging over a good spread of temperatures. It is especially difficult if it takes more than one lesson, because it can be tricky to get identical amylase concentrations on separate days.

So, there is a risk that the learning about the optimal temperature is lost, if the practical work is too fiddly and time consuming. It might be more effective, therefore, to conduct the temperature variation element as a teacher demonstration, with a set of pre-set water baths and pre-tested concentrations to ensure a good spread of times, to illustrate and cement the theoretical learning about enzyme behaviour.

If you have plenty of time, you might still decide to try this as an investigation, perhaps supplementing students' results with your own, to give them confidence in the theory and method. However, when moving on to lipases and other enzymes, having done it once for amylase, you might then do the others yourself. This saves time and provides a focus on the concepts at the appropriate moment.

Example: Exploring the efficiency of a winch system

It is possible to set up an electric winch powered by a motor, measuring the energy input using a voltmeter and ammeter and using a stop-clock to measure the time taken to raise a mass on the end of a string. The equation $E = VIt$ can be explored and reinforced. Students can then measure the energy gained by the mass when lifted a height h using $E = mgh$. The ratio of these two values leads to a calculation of the efficiency of the system.

Here, there are lots of variables to control and to measure. If we are interested primarily in generating real data for students to practise using equations, this works well as a class experiment (perhaps as part of a circus, if equipment is limited – as we discuss later). Students can experience measuring energy of different types (electrical and gravitational potential energy) and can measure the efficiency of the system directly, which is rewarding and certainly helps to reinforce the theoretical learning.

However, if you want to explore the relationship between the mass being lifted and efficiency, this becomes very difficult to do with a whole class. There are so many readings to take of all the variables that it can become overwhelming for some students. Although they could do it, they might gain just as much learning if you were to run through the process as a demonstration, perhaps using students to help, but essentially generating one set of data for everyone.

In doing so, you would free up time to plot the graph and to discuss the ideas behind the shape of the graph, the ways of defining a relationship, and so on.

By taking control of this aspect of the practical, you remove the complexity and confusion that might detract some students from the key learning point if they tried this themselves.

Example: Rates of reaction

Over the course of each student's science education, they should undertake some practical work where they control variables related to reaction rates and explore the relationships. There are some excellent, straightforward examples – such as the classic reaction between hydrochloric acid and sodium thiosulphate – that work well as class experiments.

However, if you want to explore a particular relationship in a time-efficient manner, sometimes a front-bench demonstration is a better option. A good example might be the effect of temperature on the reaction with acid and marble chips. The rate can be measured by mass lost as the CO_2 escapes.

You can carry this out with a beaker on an electronic balance, for all to see, as they record the results. By calling out the mass at regular intervals, students can each plot a graph representing the progress of the reaction, or you can plot it centrally as you go along, perhaps using Excel projected on your whiteboard, so the data entry simultaneously generates the graph.

You can then repeat the experiment with solutions at different temperatures to see how the graph shapes vary, as a means of comparing the rates of reaction. This allows you to focus on the learning about temperature and rates of reaction, instead of the intricacies of the practical arrangements and safety issues.

To be clear, there are no hard and fast rules here. The point is that you always choose the best option based on the learning you want to secure; you don't do practicals just for the sake of doing them.

Front-bench demonstrations

This mode of teaching is one of my favourites, because it allows you to drill into the detail of a range of phenomena and to generate a great sense of awe and wonder at what the students might have regarded as mundane properties of the natural world.

It is possible to get students excited about figs or bubbles of gas or repelling magnets by gathering them around you for a bit of 'show and tell' and a good discussion. Left alone with these things, they might easily dismiss the 'awe' as something ordinary.

There are a number of things to bear in mind in making a demonstration successful as a learning experience:

- Be clear in discussions with technicians about what you want set up, where and when. It is super-fiddly to get a ripple tank working just right; ask them to have it ready to go.

Science as a practical subject

- Make sure you know what you are doing with the apparatus by practising in advance. In particular, it pays to know what effect sizes and timings you are expecting. If you build the students up to expect a massive event, it can fall flat. Keep it low key if needed ... it might be a tiny, barely perceptible change they are looking for.

- Ensure that students keep a safe distance, if that is what the risk assessment dictates. You must also model maximum adherence to the safety protocols; you don't have special dispensation not to wear safety glasses.

- Take steps to maintain the students' full attention at the same time as doing the practical work yourself. This requires regular scanning, pausing for attention when needed and making sure they are arranged so that you can make eye contact with everyone if you want to. You must insist that they are not talking if you are talking, even if what you're showing them is getting them excited.

- Be clear about the key learning points you are seeking to convey through the demonstration. What are the key questions, facts and explanations?

- Ask questions during the demonstration wherever possible. It doesn't have to be a lecture.
  - What do you think is going to happen?
  - What about if we change this variable or this value?
  - Why do you think that happened?

  It might be helpful to use the think–pair–share mode of questioning while everyone has gathered around you, so that every student has to engage in what is going on and attempt to answer the questions.

- Be clear about what your expectations are in relation to what students are meant to do: should they stand, sit, write, listen, copy down results, and so on.

Something else to consider is that you can get great value from involving students in the demonstration as assistants, timekeepers, data recorders and so on. When I was training to be a teacher, feeding back after my very first observed lesson, my mentor asked: *Who was having all the fun there?*

It was me. He pointed out that I had missed opportunities to allow students to handle apparatus and play an active role. A demonstration is about the students' learning, not about the teacher having fun putting on a show for their own benefit.

I now embrace this as fully as I can, even to the point of giving full responsibility to a group of students to plan and carry out a demonstration. More simply, try as often as you can to remember: if a task can be carried out safely and efficiently by a student, let them do it instead of you.

At the end of a demonstration, engage students in activities that capture the learning as much as possible. They need to write some notes, draw diagrams, answer related questions or link the demonstration to practical work of their own. If you just leave all the ideas hanging, they will dissipate quickly. So, when planning a demonstration, you should also plan the form of the students' consolidation and practice that come next.

Class practicals

Keeping things simple, I think there are basically four types of practical work to consider:

- **A standard experiment**: this is where students know the general theory and either design a simple test or follow instructions to make observations or take measurements. Typically, students in the class would be doing the same experiment simultaneously.

- **A circus**: this is where students will complete a number of different short experiments within the lesson, rotating around the lab so that they take turns on each part of the circus.

Science as a practical subject

- **An investigation**: this is normally a more extended form of practical work where students are asked to explore relationships or phenomena by taking measurements or making observations to test out a hypothesis that, as far as they know, is not proven. It may be a hypothesis that they have proposed themselves. Here, the work of different groups will diverge, depending on the progress of their investigation.

- **A whole-class experiment**: this is where all the students contribute to collecting data that is shared as part of one experiment, where individuals can do their own analysis or everyone does it together.

Again, the decisions around which type of practical to undertake depend on the learning outcomes you are looking to secure and, to some extent, on the equipment and time you have available.

Instructions

Instructions for practical work can be provided in different ways. You need to strike a balance between giving students enough scope to make decisions, thinking for themselves about the practical set-up, and having a sufficiently positive experience so that their learning is taken forward.

Practical work can be less than satisfactory if it is too robotic, where students simply run through a recipe-style set of instructions. Similarly, if students are left floundering, without a clear idea of what to do, or have misunderstood the task, they are not going to learn as much as they could.

You can plan in advance by preparing practical guidance worksheets that are appropriately differentiated. It can help students to absorb verbal instructions if they are written down. You will find that some students find it hard to read instructions and follow them instantly, so it pays to talk them through, checking for understanding.

Here are some examples.

Standard class experiments

In these experiments, there is the possibility for learning to focus on experimental processes or on conceptual understanding, or both. You need to be clear where your emphasis lies.

- **Displacement reactions**
  Students run through a series of metal + salt-solution combinations to establish a pattern of displacement reactions and non-reactions related to the reactivity series. Handling zinc and copper sulphate solutions are important aspects of relating the theory of making observations of reactions in chemistry to macro-scale materials

  Key learning: linking pattern of observations, i.e. the vigour of the reaction, to the order of the reactivity series

  Experimental learning: making observations that enable reactions to be placed in order of vigorousness; familiarity with the materials such as copper sulphate and magnesium, linking their macro properties to their chemical behaviour

  Conceptual learning: the order of reactions is determined by the relative metal reactivity; predictions can be made on this basis

- **Energy from food**
  Burning crisps, Wotsits and crackers so that they heat water allows students to relate food energy to other forms of energy in a concrete manner. They can also have input into devising the method.

  Experimental learning: how to control variables to make it a fair test (i.e. same mass, volume of water); ideas about reliability (there are large energy losses involved) and reducing error; a more sophisticated calorimeter demonstration could be used to supplement a basic experiment involving boiling tubes and thermometers

---

Conceptual learning: energy in food varies per unit mass; stored energy can be released as heat in a measurable way

● **The standard pendulum**

This is one of the most easily controlled phenomena in physics! Students can swing a pendulum at small angles to measure the time period for different lengths of string and different masses

Experimental learning: the main learning is about the nature of relationships between variables: varying the mass does not affect the period; a null result is an important concept that arises from the experiment; simple time vs length produces a smooth-curved graph, not a straight line; data manipulation allows us to find further relationships: i.e. T^2 vs L produces a straight line through the origin of a graph

Conceptual learning: at a much higher level, the experiment can be linked to the theory of simple harmonic motion; 'g' can be measured from the gradient of the graph; however, at a lower level, the key function of this experiment is to develop learning about experimental procedures and data analysis

● **The model gut**

Students use dialysis (Visking) tubing and solutions of glucose and starch to show that the enzyme amylase breaks down starch into molecules that can pass through the semipermeable membrane of the Visking tubing

With close attention to the concentration of amylase and starch, this experiment works well. It relies on the success of finding glucose on the outside of the tubing after the amylase is added, when previously no glucose was present

This could be done as a teacher demonstration, but it is usually relatively straightforward as a class practical. It can pay off to have a 'here's one I prepared earlier' model set up, so that you can demonstrate good results in the case that your students contaminate their solutions or generally make a mess of them!

The learning about digestion is the key objective, so make sure that is the key thing they gain from it

Circus experiments

In general, a circus involves arranging a range of objects or mini experimental set-ups around the classroom. The key is to get students into groups and to send them to their initial positions. Then, after a certain amount of time, give the instruction to move around, stating the direction of movement very clearly.

If they haven't quite finished, you need to insist that they stop and move on, so that the flow of students doesn't get clogged up. It is a great way to cover a lot of ideas in a short period of time.

- **Energy transfers**
  A selection of set-ups modelling a range of energy transfers:
  - a fan blowing air towards a wind-powered generator
  - clockwork toys
  - hand-powered torches and radios
  - electric infrared heater
  - an electric motor; a Scalextric set
  - a solar cell linked to a lamp
  - a water-wheel set up in the sink, possibly linked to a generator
  - a model steam turbine
  - an electric kettle
  - some pondweed under a lamp
  - low-energy bulbs and standard filament bulbs

  The possibilities are endless, and technicians will help you with knowing what is available

Science as a practical subject

- **Food tests**

  A selection of foods are arranged at stations around the room with the appropriate food tests on hand: tests for fats, starch, proteins, glucose. Students move from station to station, conducting the tests as they go and recording their results

- **Properties of metals**

  An entry-level circus of tests for different properties of metals:

  - hardness, using a scratch test
  - flexibility and toughness
  - strength test using wires with weights added
  - electrical and thermal conductivity
  - reactions with acids and water
  - high melting points – looking at mercury samples and heating metals

  An extension of this would be to include a selection of non-metals for comparison. The idea is to carry out multiple tests in a systematic fashion, before making a summary of observations

---

ACTIVITY

In discussion with colleagues and the technicians, design a circus of experiments using the equipment in your school to explore forces, pH or plant variation – or any other topic where it could be a powerful learning experience.

Investigations

The main difference between investigations and standard experiments is that students are given the scope to determine the variables they will control and measure in order to test out a hypothesis. Normally, you would run an investigation over a few hours, spread across lessons as necessary.

Investigations work well when there are at least three input variables that can be varied or controlled. This gives rise to discussion about relative effects of different variables, as well as giving students a degree of choice.

The following list has some typical examples.

- **Rates of reaction**

  There are a number of options for reactions but two common examples are:

  reactions of marble chips (calcium carbonate) with hydrochloric acid *or* sodium thiosulphate with hydrochloric acid

  Students can investigate the effect of the concentration or the temperature of the solutions on the rate of reaction; they can explore the effect of changing the size of the marble chips

  Students can also explore using different methods to measure the rate, mass loss, time for effervescence to finish, gas collection by volume against time

  The learning is primarily around the concept of the reaction rate, but it helps for students to understand the chemistry of the reaction itself

- **Plant growth**

  The nature of plant growth requires students to set up a number of different environments in order to plot progress over a time interval of several days or weeks

  Using bean or pea seedlings, students can measure the size of specimens as they grow, placed at different distances from a light source or in water solutions with different mineral combinations

Cabomba, a pond plant, produces oxygen from photosynthesis such that it can be trapped and collected. The rate of production and the amount of oxygen collected can be used as dependent variables in an investigation

- **Potential and kinetic energy**
  Students can explore any number of experiments where energy is converted from potential to kinetic and various variables are measured and controlled:

  - Trolleys or Matchbox cars run down ramps at different heights and are then allowed to run until they stop. Distances and heights can be related to energies. Light gates can be used to measure speeds
  - Metal spheres of different masses and sizes can be dropped from a height into a sand tray. The crater size can be investigated relative to the other variables
  - Elastic-band catapults can be used to fire trolleys along a surface, exploring how far they travel for different 'pull-back' distances of the elastic band

  Experiments such as these are rich in practical and conceptual learning and allow a high degree of freedom in terms of experimental design. They also only require fairly low-cost equipment

Students should be encouraged to turn their investigations into formal reports to give a degree of rigour to the process. You don't want to spend two or three lessons where students simply play around with the equipment, without purpose.

Investigations should allow for some experimentation and decision-making, but they should have a key purpose in terms of the timescale and the written output.

Whole-class experiments

Sometimes, it is worth engaging the whole class in an experiment that you all do together. One of my favourites is measuring the speed of sound with an echo method. This requires taking the class outside a building where they can stand at least 30–40 m away from a wall.

By banging a pair of wooden blocks together sharply in rhythm with the echoes, students can take timings, such that the time for sound to travel to and from the wall can be measured. This, combined with the distance to the wall, allows students to work out the speed of sound in air.

All the students can use the same data to work out the calculations. It is a useful strategy in general to use shared data in various practicals. 'What does our data tell us?' 'Let's look at our graph.' It isn't always necessary for everyone to have their own data.

Teaching the skills

Students will encounter a range of new skills during practical lessons. These will include practical techniques, methods of measurement and analytical skills. As part of your planning for differentiation, you need to be prepared to teach these skills explicitly to some students. At the same time, it can be a good stretching experience for others to work them out for themselves.

At a basic level, the idea of a fair test, as discussed in Chapter 2, is essential. It pays to repeat this over and over: Which variables are you going to keep the same? Which *one* variable are you going to change? Which variables are you going to need to measure?

Practical skills you might need to teach include:

- using a thermometer – the issues of time delay and parallax error;

- using measuring cylinders and burettes – the meniscus issue;

- using a range of devices from metre rulers to micrometers to measure lengths and thicknesses;

- accurate timing – minimising reaction time error with a countdown method;

- how to trouble-shoot an electrical circuit (see the box below);

- reading the scale on ammeters and voltmeters;

- setting up standard equipment safely: Bunsen burner, tripod, gauze, beaker of water;

- using the tare feature on a balance so that the container mass is zeroed out.

Each of these things will be difficult for some students, or will be done sloppily. Each time you encounter a new skill, take time to teach it explicitly.

SETTING UP ELECTRICAL CIRCUITS

I find that even very able students find this challenging. You can waste a lot of time getting your students' circuits to work, before they start learning about the relationships between different variables, and so it pays to invest time in teaching self-help trouble-shooting skills.

Circuit diagrams are topological maps that show the relative position of components, but, often, there are multiple practical alternatives that produce the same outcome. It helps to make that explicit. (See Figure 7.1.)

However, in order to make life simple, my mantra is always to *make it look like the diagram*. Students should put the components in positions that match the diagrams, then add the wires and then turn the circuit on. Very often, weak connections in the wire terminals cause problems, and that is the first thing to check. With meters, it pays to put the voltmeter in last of all: the circuit should work the same, with or without the voltmeter. That is another tip.

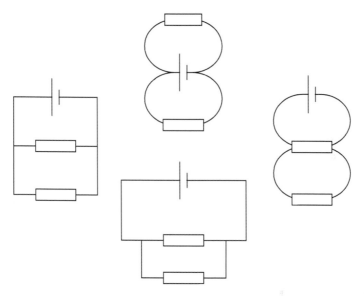

Figure 7.1 Four circuits: they look different, but they are identical

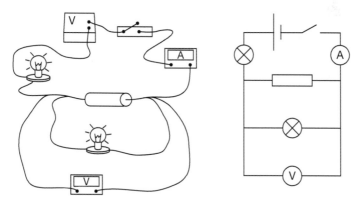

Figure 7.2 Setting up circuits to look like the diagram

Science as a practical subject

The skills of analysis also require deliberate teaching and repeated reinforcement: setting up a table of results to capture the data, repeating readings, calculating averages, using and stating the correct units, appropriate use of decimal places. Students love to copy every digit from a calculator or stopwatch; you need to show them that this is not just unnecessary – it is actually bad science.

Graphing skills require a lot of work. Students will need repeated opportunities to develop these skills. They should be learning these in maths too, and so it will pay to collaborate with your students' maths teacher to be sure you are giving the same messages.

Every aspect of graph plotting needs to be taught explicitly:

- how to determine the scale of each axis;
- the need for titles, labels and units;
- how to plot points accurately;
- sketching curves and drawing lines of best fit;
- measuring intercepts and gradients.

ACTIVITY

Prepare a model graph from a set of data similar to the set your students will gather in an experiment. Use a visualiser or projector to illustrate all the key features of excellent graphical analysis and presentation. You could also find a model example produced by a student and use this as well, or instead. The point is to show them, in advance, exactly what is expected.

As with anything, you need to establish what they can do already and then work from there. Don't assume that everyone can do something; don't assume that no one can do it either. Find out first.

Finally, you need to spend time teaching about drawing conclusions and evaluating the success of an experiment:

- What does the data tell us? Does this support the theory or prove the hypothesis?

- What level of confidence do we have that the data is accurate?

- How could the experiment have been improved to make it more reliable?

Practical write-ups

The final decision to make when planning practical work is how you want your students to record the work. For some experiments, you simply want a short summary of the observations and a sketch diagram to help your students remember what they did. If that is what you want, make it clear.

However, you will often ask students to produce a more formal write-up. If you stick to the same pattern each time, they will get into the habit of doing this and will get better at it.

A standard lab report could be framed like a standard GCSE investigation:

- Planning: a description of the hypothesis, the method and the variable being controlled.

- Observations: a table of results.

- Analysis: the graphs and any calculations and conclusions.

- Evaluation: reflections on the success of the experiment.

Alternatively, you might use a very standard format that includes: aim, method, results and conclusion.

As discussed in Chapter 4, be prepared to provide pre-made tables or writing frames for those who need it.

Science as a practical subject

Give students guidance about the style of scientific writing. The expected style in most situations is to use the third person:

The apparatus was set up as shown in the diagram. Temperatures were recorded at minute intervals, taking care to stir the solution throughout.

The graph shows that the acceleration of the trolley was directly proportional to the force applied.

You may prefer a less formal style, but take care to challenge informal, anecdotal reports:

Well, first of all, Mr Jones said to get the equipment. Daisy did the timing while I dropped the ball. I think we needed to work faster because we ran out of time at the end.

This style of writing has its place, but it isn't appropriate in scientific contexts, including exams. Your department may have a policy on this.

Make the connections

Practical work is extremely rewarding as a learning experience in itself. Experiments are real problem-solving situations that give great satisfaction. However, there are loftier goals.

The most important reason for doing practical work in science is to reinforce the core philosophical underpinning of the subject. The scientific ideas that become accepted over time are those that can be shown to explain the measurable, observable world that we live in. They allow us to make predictions that can be tested.

Making connections from abstract ideas about atoms, molecules and energy to real events that we can see for ourselves is hugely rewarding, but also vitally important. The domains of theory and experiment are mutually reinforcing at a conceptual level and a philosophical level.

So, science is very much a practical subject. Make sure that your students experience it that way.

TALKING POINTS

1 Which experiments might secure better conceptual understanding if you do them as demonstrations instead of class practicals?
2 Where are there opportunities for students to do open-ended investigations, where they establish relationships or make observations for themselves, as a 'discovery learning' experience?
3 What level of caution is required so that risks are mitigated, without making science seem risk and danger free, losing some of its capacity to inspire awe and wonder?

8 Formative assessment

Assessment is a core component of great teaching. You need to know how well your students are doing; they need to know how well they are doing for themselves. Above all, they need to know how to improve: how to deepen their understanding of science and how to demonstrate their knowledge and understanding more effectively.

Formative assessment is a term for the numerous ways in which you can determine how well students have understood the science they are learning, leading to feedback that helps them to improve.

You will encounter the term 'assessment for learning' (AfL) in this context. For a variety of reasons, this term is increasingly problematic, as it is often misused, and it has become a piece of educational jargon that can be a barrier. Formative assessment is a much better way to describe the principle and practice of giving feedback, based on students' performance in demonstrating their learning, in order to secure improvement.

There are a number of important types of formative assessment that you are likely to use:

- oral feedback
- marking – or written feedback
- self-assessment

- peer assessment

- formative use of tests.

Before exploring these in detail, it is helpful to consider some of the difficulties with assessment and feedback in general.

Learning is invisible

- How well does Jack understand the concept of homeostasis?

- Does Sabrina understand the difference between refraction and diffraction?

- How well does Harun know the structural features of hydro-carbons, esters and alcohols?

- Does Sam know exactly what DNA is and what genes are?

Unless we engage in an appropriate form of assessment, we cannot know these things; we can't see how each student has formulated their ideas in their minds. If we don't know, then we can't plan the next steps in our teaching in a precise manner. However, any form of assessment requires some kind of student performance; it is the performance that we see, and not the learning itself.

In practice, it means that, when we set up any assessment, we need to recognise that the performance we see is only an approximation to the learning; it may over- or understate the true level of understanding. There is error and uncertainty in any assessment, and that is worth bearing in mind.

Grades and scores don't necessarily help students to improve

If our goal was to improve students' understanding, then what would be the value of giving a piece of work a grade? A C grade, an A, or perhaps a B+? This approach to assessment is an attempt to judge the standard of the work. The implication of a B+ is that the work could have been better. It is also better than a B and much better than a C. However, that is not very helpful. What students need to know is how their work could be improved. Grades by themselves don't do this.

Scores are the same: 16 out of 20, 3 out of 5 or 83 per cent are different ways of telling you how much you got right compared with full marks. The scores don't tell you where you went wrong, what you did well or how to improve further still.

In both cases, students need to know what scores and grades mean in terms of the work itself, with opportunities to then improve their work to seek a higher score or grade at the next attempt. The information from the assessment, the feedback, is what they need, not the grade or score itself.

Praise is not formative

Well done, Very good, Excellent, Brilliant, ✓ ✓, ☺.

We all like a bit of encouragement from time to time. It is reassuring, and that isn't a bad thing. Praise can help to generate an engaged, positive classroom atmosphere and can build self-esteem. However, it doesn't directly help us to improve, especially if we are not exactly sure why we are being praised.

Praise can be useful, if we know what the praise is for. 'That's a really good graph John, because you've got all the axes labelled, the scales are plotted so that the data is well spread and the line is a smooth curve, through most of the points.'

Praise, used in this specific way, can reinforce learning and the standards you are trying to set.

It is hard to aim at something you can't see or define

Jack writes an answer explaining the idea of transpiration. However, he doesn't know how well he is supposed to understand transpiration. When writing his answer, how would he know whether he's reached the required standard?

Is it enough, at Jack's level, to talk about water being absorbed from moisture in the soil by root hair cells and escaping from the leaves? Or, does he need to talk about osmosis, concentration gradients and diffusion?

Jack needs a clear idea of the level at which to pitch his answer and then some process by which he can measure how close he is to the standard he was aiming for. He needs some guide as to what a really good answer might look like for someone at his stage in the learning.

Simply knowing you need to get from A to B doesn't help you make the journey

Alicia has written an explanation of how a kidney works. Her answer scores 3 out of 8. Her friend Daisy produced a model answer worth 8 out of 8. But, how did Daisy know what to write? If Alicia had known what to write, she would have written it . . . she can see where she is and where Daisy is, but how is she going to get there too?

Here, the task is to break it down into steps. Most areas of science have a logical flow of concepts that build up, telling the story from observation to theory and back again. Alicia needs to find a way to tell that story, one piece at a time.

Formative assessment is the overarching term for the processes we use to address these issues. Much of the current thinking in this area originated from the work of Dylan Wiliam and Paul Dyson, in their groundbreaking pamphlet, 'Inside the black box' (1990), which is well worth reading.

Originally, they coined the phrase 'assessment for learning' to distinguish their ideas from the assessment 'of learning' – the practice of merely measuring how well students performed at the end of a unit of work, without letting them learn from the process. However, Dylan Wiliam has since suggested that 'formative assessment' is a better term.

Formative assessment

Essentially, formative assessment has **four** components:

Firstly, learners need to establish where they are in their knowledge and understanding. 'What do I know already?' 'What is it that I don't fully understand?'

Then, they need to establish clearly where they want to go. 'What are the standards or skill levels I am aiming for?'

They then need to know how to get to the learning goal from where they are. 'What, exactly, do I need to do now to make progress?'

Finally, they need to attempt to make the journey – they need to act on the feedback. 'I will act on that information and advice and use it to do a better job this time.'

Another way to express this is as follows:

- Find out what students can do already; then, set a goal for the learning they are trying to secure, attempting to be ambitious and realistic.
- Engage students in tasks that help them progress towards that goal.
- Assess their learning to see how close they are to reaching the goal.
- Give them feedback as to where they are and what they still need to improve.
- Engage in further tasks; assess them again and give more feedback.
- Repeat as often as necessary.
- Eventually the goal will be reached.

To illustrate this, I often find it useful to think of a process that is easy to define: the long jump. To coach an athlete to maximise their success in the long jump, you would do the following things:

- Measure how far they could jump already.
- Set a goal for them to try to reach: something realistic but ambitious.

- Give some specific feedback about how to improve – the technique of long jump.

- Observe them act on that feedback and measure their success.

- Give further feedback, reinforcing what they are doing right and suggesting the specific aspects of the technique that need improving.

In this example, it is no good just to say, 'Well done, great, have another go' or 'No, that is not good enough, work harder'.

The ideal form of feedback is both **positive** and **specific**:

Well done, your jumps have improved. To increase the distance further you need to push off from the board with that leading leg and keep your chin well forward. Try that next time and see if you can make 5 metres.

I have used this example because both the goals and the athlete's attainment are immediately obvious. Formative assessment in science follows the same model, but, first, you need to do some work do define the attainment goals, or **learning objectives**. To do this, it is often very useful to use **success criteria**.

Learning objectives

I often feel that, if I have planned a good lesson, the learning objectives are very clear. I know very clearly what my students should try to learn. In planning your lessons, you should try to design them around meeting the objectives, rather than around tasks.

For example, good learning objectives might be:

- to understand that the liver contains natural catalysts that speed up digestion;

- to understand the relationship between chain length and viscosity in hydrocarbons;

- to be able to calculate acceleration and distance travelled from a velocity–time graph.

Formative assessment

These are specific objectives that you can use to gauge students' understanding and the progress they've made. They are statements that can be tested by asking questions or setting some form of assessment.

Less effective objectives tend to focus on tasks: 'Complete the onion cell microscope practical and do questions 5 and 6 on page 8.' This is not a learning objective; it is just a 'to do' list. All you can do with it is check that students have done it or not; it can't help you or your students clarify what the key learning points are or how well they've done.

Try to get into the habit of identifying one or two very clear learning objectives for each lesson. It is helpful to share this with students, either orally or by writing it down. However, don't feel you need to write learning objectives on the board for every single lesson. It becomes monotonous, and often students do it mechanically without really engaging with the content.

In keeping with the 'teach to the top' approach that I advocate, I would stick to one key objective for everyone in the class, something that is challenging for the ablest. This means everyone is aiming high. Setting lower expectations in your learning objectives for some students isn't something I recommend; differentiation is about helping the weaker students to reach the top, not setting their sights low.

To consolidate the learning in a lesson and to help you plan the next steps, you can wrap up a lesson by assessing how students have done in relation to the learning objectives.

For example, you could ask students to write an answer in their books or on a mini-whiteboard that captures the essence of the learning in hand:

- Learning objective: to understand how the focal length of an eye lens is adjusted for near and distant objects.

- Review question: in bullet points, explain how the eye is controlled to focus on a near object and then a distant object.

Students write the answers on their whiteboards and raise them all simultaneously. You scan the answers looking for model exemplars and some that are slightly off or wrong, giving feedback accordingly.

Alternatively, you could ask students to write their answers on Post-it notes or scrap paper that you collect as they leave the lesson. This 'exit question' approach gives you time to digest the information about how well they've done, in order to plan your next lesson.

ACTIVITY

For some of the lessons you have planned, write down the learning objectives you will have in mind and then consider what effective review questions would look like that would tell you if a student had met the objectives.

Success criteria

Another way to establish desired learning outcomes or standards for students' work is to use a set of success criteria. For example, you might set criteria for your expectations of students' practical reports. You can do this yourself, or it can be very powerful to involve students in helping to agree the success criteria with you.

OK, what should we be looking for in an excellent practical report?

An aim for the experiment? *Yes . . . or we could call it a hypothesis.*

A good clear diagram. *Yes – that along with a simple explanation of the method.*

A graph. *OK . . . but what would make the graph an excellent graph?*

Units on the axes, labels and a smooth curve through the points. *Agreed.*

Formative assessment

> A conclusion? *Yes . . . what might we look for in a conclusion?*
>
> Saying what the graph looks like. *Is that all . . . what about the hypothesis?*
>
> Saying how well the graph matches the hypothesis? *Good . . . we're getting there.*

You are asking them to recall prior knowledge; you are giving them a chance to have a say, but you are also steering them towards higher expectations and more tightly focused goals.

To help with marking and feedback, it is often very useful to produce a grid that reflects the agreed success criteria. It also helps students to deliver the best work they can.

Year 8 practical report success criteria		
Criteria	Comment	Redraft
A well-structured hypothesis that can be tested in the experiment		
A graph with labelled axes, title, units and all points plotted correctly		
A conclusion that links the results to the hypothesis, using the correct scientific language and reasoning		

The ideal scenario is when students receive feedback on the criteria and then have the opportunity to act on the feedback to produce an improved draft. This can then be commented on. If you give feedback that is not acted on, most of it will be lost, and students won't necessarily remember it the next time they do an experiment.

Success criteria can be used for any number of open-ended tasks:

- producing a PowerPoint presentation;
- making a website;
- writing an article for a scientific journal.

In each case, it is possible for students to aim too low, unless they know the expected standards. Using success criteria can help you and your students to understand exactly how high to aim.

YEAR 10 PHYSICS: ENERGY TRANSFER PRESENTATIONS

Students are asked to prepare a short presentation on a specific energy transfer. They have been given success criteria for the task that include presentational features – clear, loud voice, keeping to time – and content: use correct terms for each form of energy and discuss any energy losses.

The presentations are short, so that several can be seen in 20 minutes. The teacher then asks them to self-assess against the criteria, having seen the other presentations. He stresses the need for vocal projection and the need to be specific about types of potential energy and not to confuse force and energy.

The students then redo their presentations, taking on the general advice and their own self-assessment. The second time around, they are much better; the science is better explained.

Here, the re-run helps students to capitalise on the feedback and to engage with the criteria more accurately, having seen how well or badly other groups performed.

Mark schemes as criteria

It can be difficult to define precise criteria for every single aspect of science. 'Getting the answers right' might be obvious, but often there are several good alternatives. In common with public examinations, using a mark scale is a useful way to suggest the level of difficulty or depth of answer you expect.

A 2-mark answer is different to a 4-, 6- or 8-mark answer. Examiners use precise mark schemes to help give consistent marks, and this is a technique you can use too. You can give students the mark scheme, or ask them to write the mark scheme with you as an exercise.

Q: How do animals gain energy from food?

This question can be answered on many levels, and so the mark scheme approach can help to make this clear. Simply by knowing it is a 5-mark answer, students will pitch their responses accordingly, instead of just going for a simple one-line attempt.

The mark scheme might include marks for: explaining food types as stores of chemical energy, the role of digestion, absorption of molecules of simple carbohydrates into the bloodstream, storage of carbohydrates and fat as energy store, the respiration process in cells, and knowing the respiration equation.

At different levels, the mark scheme will tell students what to expect in terms of the range and depth of the concepts they need to include. With repeated practice, they will get better at pitching appropriate answers.

Exemplars

Another very powerful way to show students what you are looking for is to show them examples. For example, if you have a perfect graph, showing all the features you want and using the correct techniques, show this to the class. It is especially effective if one of the students in that class (or a similar class from last year) produced the exemplar.

One of the best bits of kit to have available for this purpose is a **visualiser**. This can be bought as a stand-alone item, linked to a projector, or it could be a webcam, or the camera on an iPad or mobile phone.

If you capture a student's work and project it on the screen as a model for others to follow, it is very effective. I've used this for showing exemplary answers to exam questions, exemplary calculations and exemplary explanations of phenomena shown in the lessons.

The key is to focus on *why* the work is good, not just to give praise and encouragement.

- Example of teacher response: Let's look at Jacob's answer. It got full marks. He set out the advantages of the cloning method, with an example; then he's given a good disadvantage, looking at the ethical issues. Then he has concluded by suggesting the benefits outweigh the disadvantages, with a reason.

- Example of using exemplars created in a lesson: Groups of Year 11 students have been asked to plot graphs from data gained from a rates-of-reaction experiment. A range of numerical skills are needed to scale the axes. In order to gauge success, each group's graph is shared on the visualiser and discussed. Success criteria are agreed for the quality of the graphs and their interpretation; the next graphs produced are far superior.

The other function of using exemplars is not just to show students what is correct, but also to show them what is possible. If you have some outstanding pieces of work from students that demonstrate clarity of thinking or exceptional effort, going far beyond the requirements of a research project, then keep them to inspire other students to follow.

Having established clear criteria for success, the most important aspect of formative assessment is giving feedback.

Oral feedback

Excellent oral feedback is the bread and butter of great teaching. It is closely linked to oral questioning, described in Chapter 6. In my experience, giving sharply focused oral feedback is very often the best way to explain the nuances of how an answer can be improved.

In very simple terms, the positive–specific format is the ideal.

The rabbit–owl population graph is under discussion.

OK, what is happening and why?

The rabbit population goes down because the owls are eating them.

That's true for this part of the graph. Good. But you need to describe the whole graph, using two or three sentences. Also, find a better way to say 'goes down' or 'eats', and let's use the predator–prey terminology.

At first, the rabbit population decreases, because they are consumed by predators, the owls. As the number of rabbits decreases, there is less food for the owls to eat so their population starts to drop. Then the rabbit population can increase again because there are fewer owls.

Well done. That is a much better answer, because you have explained the whole cycle and shown that both populations interact over time, using the terminology correctly.

After some oral feedback like this, you can then push the student to develop their thinking further with another probing question.

If you have used a whole-class response system, such as the mini-whiteboards described in Chapter 6, then you need to make sure you respond to the range of answers presented. You don't have to respond to every single answer; try to select examples of good answers, interesting answers and slightly incorrect answers.

If an answer is correct, saying, 'Good, well done', isn't necessarily helpful. You can go further with, 'That's correct, why did you put that? How did you work it out?'. Very often, this is the most important part of the learning: how you work out the answer is more useful than knowing a specific answer.

If an answer is incorrect, you can use it as an opportunity to make wrong answers part and parcel of the learning process: 'That's not quite right, but what were you thinking? How did you get that answer? OK, I see why you said that, but now think about whether the rabbit population could grow forever? What would limit the population?'

As far as possible, turn a wrong answer into a learning opportunity for the whole class.

Written feedback (marking)

Oral feedback is immensely powerful, but you can't really ask every single student a series of questions in a lesson context and give feedback on their answers orally. This is where marking comes in.

Stereotypical, old-fashioned marking is where the teacher makes a series of ticks and crosses in red pen on a piece of work and then gives a grade, say a B+, with a comment such as 'Could do better' or 'Very good'.

The main issue with this type of approach is that it is not formative; it tells the student that they have some room for improvement, but it doesn't help them to do it. The student doesn't

Formative assessment

know why they got an answer wrong, why a paragraph deserves a tick or why they got a B+ and not an A- or a plain B.

The same is true of giving scores for assignments or classwork. If a piece of writing or set of questions gains 14/20, it indicates that there were 6 marks-worth of mistakes or omissions. Left alone, without further comment, that isn't any use to the student.

Marking formatively is a different process altogether. Increasingly, schools are adopting 'comments only' marking policies. Instead of using grades, teachers simply write comments. The theory is that students will not read comments if they have a grade, but, if they only receive comments, they are more likely to engage with them.

Effective written comments can have a simple pattern to them:

* some words of encouragement;
* some features that are good and should be sustained;
* some specific errors to correct;
* some areas to improve on or to explore further.

For example:

Harun, You've done well, tackling some of the harder questions. I like your explanation of the aluminium extraction process; you have understood the sequence well. You need to look again at Questions 3 and 4 where the equations are not balanced correctly. Also try to include a reference to the electrodes, saying which is positive and negative.

This kind of comment can be supported by annotations on the work. Ticks and crosses are well-understood symbols, but they need to be explained further.

Marking can become a massive burden for teachers, unless they manage it well and are realistic about it. When you take in your students' exercise books to do some marking, bear the following things in mind:

Be selective: It is not possible to give written feedback on every piece of work a student produces, checking every single answer to every question and every spelling error. It is better to focus on certain, selected pieces of work, marking them thoroughly and asking students to make improvements.

It is better still if you highlight clearly which pieces of work students will self-assess and which pieces you will be taking in to mark yourself. This helps to manage expectations.

Be focused: Students can't always respond to every comment you make; there is only so much they can take in at once, so don't overload them. If a piece of work is covered in red pen, it is difficult for the student to know how to respond; very often, they won't respond at all, unless you make this easy and clear. The solution is to highlight a small number of corrections they should make, including the key spelling errors.

Use well-understood codes: It is helpful to teach your students a set of feedback codes that you will use in your marking. Sometimes, schools have an agreed set across a department.

The strategy is then to apply the codes in your marking, forcing your students to engage with their work to identify the issues and to respond to them.

Common codes might indicate:

- a factual error that should be checked;
- an incomplete answer that needs more depth;
- a statement that has not been explained;
- a spelling error;
- missing units;
- a calculation error;
- presentational issues, with titles missing;
- poorly drawn straight lines or curves.

Formative assessment

If students know your shorthand for these issues, it makes marking much easier for you. However, it also forces them to think and to engage with the feedback at a deeper level.

Marking is a powerful form of differentiation. Some students will need more help than others. They will need direct guidance and a clear structure to help them improve:

> Photosynthesis: Photo-SYN-thesis. Try to learn this spelling.

> Perhaps start with: As the concentration INCREASES, the time for the reaction . . .

Others will just need hints, clues and prompts.

> Is there a better way to explain this using energy instead of force?

> Does this happen in every case?

> Have you taken account of the initial temperature?

> There is a big error in this paragraph. Can you spot it?

If you keep the workload to a manageable level, selective marking is an excellent way to engage with your students' learning and to get to know them. Very often, quieter students reveal their learning far more clearly in their written work than they manage to do in the verbal exchanges in the class.

Peer and self-assessment

Used in conjunction with marking and oral feedback, it is extremely effective to engage students in marking their own work and the work of others. In practice, it also saves a lot of time. However, you need to teach students to assess their work properly, so you can use it to maximum effect.

Self-assessment, where the students evaluate their own work, and peer assessment, where students check the work of others, can use the same techniques:

- checking against a set of correct answers; some textbooks have answers in the back, and it is a very straightforward process for students to see which answers they got right or wrong;

- applying the success criteria that were agreed prior to a task being set;

- checking against a detailed mark scheme, such as with examination papers.

In all of these processes, the main focus should be on identifying areas of confusion, misconceptions and errors, so that you can address them in the lesson. Focusing on 'wrong answers' so that this is normal and routine is a good way to encourage students to take a few risks, to make an attempt, even when they are unsure of themselves.

If it is done well, peer and self-assessment helps to teach students the science, but it also gives them an insight into the nature of assessment and the structure of good answers.

The biology class is preparing for an examination with very specific guidelines for '6-mark answers' in response to questions about public health:

> Some people believe that alcohol is a drug and should be treated as one. Do you agree?

Instead of writing answers directly, they first write a **mark scheme** for the question. They then write their answer, swap with a partner and use their own mark scheme to evaluate, **peer assess** and give a mark out of six to their partner, with associated feedback.

The feedback is then acted on to secure improvements. This process leads to very strong responses, combining an interest in the question itself with a deeper understanding of the assessment process.

For the sake of time-efficiency and to give genuine value to the students' own assessments, it isn't sensible to routinely double-check work that has been peer or self-assessed. Over the course of a series of lessons, if you mark some work and students assess the rest, you'll be getting the balance right.

Formative use of summative tests

Tests are an excellent way to generate formative feedback. However, you need to make sure you create time in the lesson sequence to make this work. If you set a test at the end of a topic and give students their marks just prior to moving on to the next topic, you've missed an opportunity for students to learn.

If Alex knows he got 62 per cent on a test, it doesn't help him to understand science any better; he just knows he got some answers wrong. He might also be able to compare himself with the others in the class, but, again, that isn't much use to him.

However, if you create the time for it, tests can provide a rich source of feedback. The test papers will show each student where their weaknesses are, and the overall results will help you to gain an overview of the common errors and misconceptions.

Ideally, you should time a test to be part way through a unit of work, allowing you to use subsequent lessons to follow up afterwards. Give students the opportunity to improve answers and to make corrections, and give yourself a chance to explain certain concepts more clearly, if necessary.

Closing the gap: acting on feedback

There is a growing recognition that feedback in itself is not sufficient. The final stage in the formative feedback process is that students need to act on it. The process of acting on feedback to secure improvement can be called 'closing the gap'. Read this blog post: http://headguruteacher.com/2012/11/10/mak-feedback-count-close-the-gap/, for an account of the work being done at Saffron Walden High School, where this idea originated.

This means closing the gap between the student's initial efforts and the standard they could reach if they acted on all the feedback. They may have received feedback orally, from your marking or from their own self-assessment, but it won't have made much difference if they don't act on it straight away.

This means:

- redrafting answers to gain as close to full marks as possible;
- making corrections to spelling errors or factual inaccuracies;
- redrawing graphs with more accurate points or lines;
- correcting calculation errors and adding missing units;
- rewriting numbers with an appropriate number of significant figures.

Ideally, you will give students time to do this immediately after giving them the feedback. When you hand out the books you have just marked, you must give the class time to reflect on the feedback and to improve their work accordingly. It is a very good use of time.

If you allow students to routinely hand in shoddy work, with lots of mistakes that are not addressed, then you'll be setting low expectations and losing credibility. If you insist on students continually improving, using homework and class time until their work is at the required standard, you will become regarded as a strong teacher who sets high standards.

Over time, students will try to live up to your expectations. So, set them as high as possible.

TALKING POINTS

1 How will you communicate the standards that you expect in terms of the work that should be completed, the depth of answers required and the quality of written work?
2 How will you manage your marking so that you can be sure that all your students will act on the feedback, 'closing the gap', without creating an unreasonable workload?
3 What information do you need to give in your oral feedback or in your written marking to secure improvement?

9 Getting your first job

The first step in getting a teaching job is to look at the types of school you're interested in and to aim for the jobs that you'd genuinely like to have. You might have a preference for working in a non-denominational mixed comprehensive, a girls' school, a faith school or some other particular type of school.

Very often, head teachers are looking for people committed to their type of school. Although that isn't always the case, it is sensible to know the background and to be able to talk sensibly about the value of comprehensive education, single-sex education or a faith-based ethos, as appropriate.

You might be determined to teach A level as well as GCSE, but, equally, you might be happy to work in an 11–16 school. A key issue for science teachers is whether you'll be expected to teach general science, or whether you're more likely to be asked to teach physics, chemistry or biology as a separate subject.

In weighing these things up, I'd recommend being open-minded. Your first job is likely to be the first of many; over time, you can move around and work in different school contexts. The most important consideration early on is whether you'll be able to work in an environment that allows you to grow and develop as a science teacher, and that is true of most schools.

Before you start applying for jobs, it is important to recognise that recruitment is a two-way process; it is more akin to matchmaking than a straight contest. Head teachers will want people who will enjoy working in their school; I always say that it's hard to get a job you don't really want. If you have doubts or if you are half-hearted, it shows.

Once you've found a job that seems attractive, the aim of your application and interview is to do two things:

- Firstly, you need to show that you could be a great science teacher. No one will expect you to be the finished article; at this stage, it is about showing your potential.

- Secondly, you also need to demonstrate how well suited you'd be to the specific job on offer. Different schools and roles have niche requirements that you need to tune in to. It pays to give the application your all, focusing on each school separately, rather than using a generic application for lots of jobs at once.

What does the ideal candidate look like?

As a head, I have been involved in hundreds of interviews and read thousands of application forms. Really, there is no ideal candidate; everyone is different, and there is no mould for an outstanding teacher. However, there are certain things I'd be looking for from prospective candidates:

They understand teaching and learning and talk about them with knowledge and passion. They can articulate what a great lesson might look like, what an effective series of lessons might require, and how students can engage in the process to maximise their learning outcomes. I want it all: rigour, challenge, joyfulness, passion, solid dependability, originality and flair – and I'll look for the best I can find.

They have a strong knowledge base, including subject know-ledge, approaches to pedagogy, important policy issues – including recent changes – and effective assessment practices. As well as their responses at interview, their record of training, their academic background and the range of their relevant professional experience will influence my assessment.

I want someone other colleagues might learn from, and someone the students will be inspired by. This could be an NQT or a more experienced teacher. Preferably, I want someone who offers flexibility in terms of subject teaching and other activities, but that is icing on the cake.

They have positive attitudes towards students and parents and show a willingness to embrace the idea of inclusion and the prospect of teaching more able learners. They project a general aura of professionalism and the capacity to work effectively in a team. I can live with a few solo operators, but, ideally, I want people who value collegiality.

Enthusiasm goes a long way, but obviously isn't enough on its own. I want people who will go the 'extra mile'. This isn't a case of selling your soul; it's a legitimate expectation. Schools rely on people contributing to the community beyond the classroom, doing whatever it takes to support some individuals and taking professional development seriously.

They are willing to learn. However well qualified or experienced someone is, I still want to know they are able to take advice, to try new ideas and to strive to develop continually. Sometimes, applicants can appear too eager to show they know everything already, when they'd do better to project a humbler disposition, with evidence of continuing academic or professional learning.

They have personal presence, appearing assertive and confident, but with a bit of humility, charm and humour; they would be someone you can imagine working well with students and staff, prepared to challenge students and colleagues if necessary, but also able to form warm, positive relationships. They may have areas to develop, but you can imagine them being able to secure excellent behaviour in their lessons.

Their career history supports what you see. Ideally, I want evidence of success in some aspect of an applicant's life. I'm interested in interesting people – variety is really healthy – but I need a good explanation for someone who has been chopping and changing. If you've been moving jobs or colleges year after year, or appear to have been static, doing one job in one place, it can raise questions.

If people have a complex story to tell, I want them to tell it, not expect me to piece it together. People enter the profession and can become superb teachers with all kinds of career background; most heads are very open-minded, but it helps to know the story.

They have leadership capacity or potential ... Of course, the teaching role will be the most important, but, ideally, I want people who might be able to take on some leadership responsibilities in the future. I'd be looking for people who can analyse problems and offer solutions, have a vision for what could be achieved in science education, and have the power to motivate others and the organisational skills to back it up.

Taking all of this on board, the recruitment process is all about working out how well each candidate fits. Each school will have a similar list. **So, how do you show you're the person they're looking for?**

Before you apply

In order to give yourself the best chance of being selected for a job as a science teacher, think about the experience and interests that you have, and how they might come across. If you think about it well in advance, you have time to build up your profile in readiness, filling in obvious gaps.

You should consider some of the following:

- enrolling with the Association of Science Education or subject organisations, such as the Royal Society of Chemists or the Institute of Physics;

- undertaking a Masters course or some form of post-graduate study;

- seeking out opportunities to spend time in schools as an observer or teaching assistant; the more time you can spend in schools, the better;

- getting involved with youth organisations that give you experience of working with young people and developing the skills you'll need in the classroom;

- reading contemporary books about science or about education in general, so that you are familiar with current issues and the relevant terminology;

- signing up for Twitter and following the wide range of teachers who write blogs and share ideas about education online.

Application forms

On a very practical level, you need to take time to fill in the forms very thoroughly, making sure that someone who doesn't know you can get the full picture of your education, qualifications and employment history. Take great care not to undermine your credibility with spelling errors.

The most difficult part is writing the personal statement. This is often restricted to two sides of A4 as a maximum. I usually suggest that people pick out four or five areas from the person specification and set out separate paragraphs for each one. You should aim to do two things:

1 Set out your ideas for teaching and what you'd like to contribute in each area.

2 Provide examples to show that you have the capacity to be successful, based on your past experience.

You might want to include a selection of areas, such as:

- effective teaching and learning;

- securing strong examination outcomes;

- behaviour management;
- formative assessment;
- differentiation and inclusion;
- curriculum planning and innovation;
- engaging in pastoral support and the wider school community;
- extracurricular activities.

There is a danger in trying to write too much, over-egging your past glories and bragging unnecessarily. Avoid writing a long list of everything you've ever done, and drop anything that is ancient history, even if it sounds impressive.

Don't just write a list of what you will do in the future, without any evidence that you know what you're doing based on past experience. Try to show that you know about the school by making reference to the syllabus used or some of the recent events or successes shown on the school website.

Application pitfalls include spelling mistakes, mentioning the wrong school, unexplained gaps in employment, unexplained departures from jobs, bad handwriting, no mention of teaching and learning, and overly soppy platitudes about loving children and wanting to change lives.

Interviews

No two processes are the same, but they normally include common elements:

- an observed lesson;
- a panel interview with students;
- a panel interview with senior staff and possibly some governors.

In preparing for an interview, it is wise to think through potential questions in advance, so that you don't appear surprised by them.

Classic interview questions

'Give us an example of . . .'

- a lesson you've taught recently that was a success. (This could be from a teaching practice placement.) Why was it successful and how could you tell? How could you improve it?
- a situation that you found challenging which you then overcame;
- an individual student or a class that you have had particular success with;
- an initiative that you have led involving other people;
- a successful approach to raising achievement/improving attendance/improving behaviour that you've been involved in.

The examples you choose need to be tailored to the school you're applying to. Make it as relevant as possible. For example, don't focus on your lower-achieving C/D borderline group, if the school wants a top-end A/A* A level teacher, and vice versa.

Prepare these answers in advance, but adjust to the nuances of what you pick up at the school you're going to. Clearly, the more real experience you have of these things, the easier it will be to give good answers. For example, a 'challenging situation' could relate to an issue at your football club, but you dealt with it; it was real, and you learned something. That is far better than talking only about hypothetical future scenarios.

Other common questions

- What are the key challenges facing teachers/facing this school/ facing young people/in your subject?
- How would your colleagues/students/current employer describe you?
- What are your strengths/greatest achievements?
- What are your areas for development?

Getting your first job

- Why do you want to work at this particular school?
- How could data be used effectively to support you as a teacher?
- How can you engage 'hard to reach' families?

The data issue is all about making sure you know your students very well, using patterns of attainment to set high expectations, to monitor progress and to give feedback. Data should help you take actions to refocus learning at a classroom level. There is no correct answer on 'hard to reach' families, but you need to have some ideas about engaging families with the learning and making regular contact, for positive reasons as well as negative.

Across your answers, show you are aware of SEN issues and child protection procedures and try to mention the role of parents. Think in terms of good systems and the fact that people are in teams and shouldn't work in isolation.

You're likely to be asked about safeguarding. The key things are to listen to what children tell you, always be open to the possibility that some form of abuse explains their behaviour, never promise confidentiality to a child, gather factual information without asking leading questions and involve the named child protection officer if you have even the slightest concern.

Some of the **interview pitfalls** that might undermine you include the following:

Bad first impressions: looking scruffy, top button undone, a dirty, crumpled shirt (arguably superficial, but why risk suggesting that you don't care, for a job you want), giggling or being humourlessly unsmiling, not making eye contact, being over-familiar (I might offer, 'please, call me Tom', . . . but don't presume), fussing and worrying about the details of the day.

During the interview:

- Giving answers that are too short suggests a lack of depth. Try to be expansive, giving fully extended answers. Use notes if you have to, rather than walking out with half your ideas unsaid.

- Giving answers that are too long is offputting. Read the signals and respect the timing of the process. This applies to presentations too. If you're told you have 10 minutes, don't give them 15. It can give an unintended message.

- Being out of date: If the SEN legislation has changed, and you're talking about the old framework, you're on a loser. Make sure you are well versed in the latest version of the science National Curriculum and the GCSE requirements.

- Talking excessively about stress, workload, difficulties, problems, barriers, etc.: We know about these things; in the interview, you need to focus on how to overcome them.

- Talking about yourself, without reference to the team: Even if you are going for a first teaching job, try to show an awareness of the fact that you will be forming part of a team; that you will share resources, seek advice and offer support as required.

Interview lessons

The secret to these lessons is to keep them simple. Try to select one or two key ideas that you want to explain in your lesson and focus on them. If you are given a choice, opt for something challenging.

A typical structure of an interview lesson would be:

- a brisk introduction of yourself and the key learning objective;
- some teaching input from you, perhaps with a pre-prepared resource or PowerPoint of high quality;
- a short discussion activity in pairs or groups;
- a structured question and answer exchange, where you model some formative assessment methods and probing questioning;
- another task that involves some thinking, writing or problem-solving;
- a final review or reporting back from some of the groups to wrap it up;
- concluding by referring back to your original learning objective.

During the lesson, make sure you ask for students' names, be assertive and friendly, but always challenge off-task talking. Keep an eye on the timing and aim to finish crisply.

Interview lesson pitfalls: overrunning; talking far too much before the students do anything themselves; pitching the material too high or too low; allowing off-task chat to continue without any challenge; being timid; wasting time moving the furniture or giving out over-elaborate resources; not having a clear enough objective to assess against within the time frame; not challenging errors and misconceptions; not responding to answers, especially if students already know more than you expected.

Ultimately, it is a competition. There are hundreds of factors, and employers are generally well motivated and keen to get the best people they can. If you are unsuccessful, ask for feedback and learn from it. There will be a period of dejection after a rejection, but, keep going, keep expanding your repertoire of experience and, ultimately – if you learn from the feedback – a chance may come along where you fit the bill.

Finally . . .

I've been working in education for more than 25 years now. It's a wonderfully rewarding career. I've taken on a range of posts of responsibility, from head of year to assistant head and deputy head, and I've been a head teacher for several years now. However, it's still true that, when a stranger asks me what I do for a living, I say I'm a science teacher. That's the part I love the most, and I'm proud to say it every time. I hope you will be too.

Good luck!

Bibliography

Association for Science Education (2010) *The Language of Measurement: Terminology Used in School Science Investigations*, Hatfield: Association for Science Education.

Barton, G. (2013) *Don't Call it Literacy!* Abingdon: Routledge.

Berger, R. (2003) *An Ethic of Excellence*, Portsmouth: Heinemann.

Black, P. and Wiliam, D. (1990) 'Inside the black box: raising standards through classroom assessment', London: Kings College London.

Bryson, B. (2010) *A Short History of Nearly Everything*, London: Random House.

Carey, J. (ed.) (1995) *The Faber Book of Science*, London: Faber and Faber.

Dawkins, R. (2005) *The Ancestor's Tale*, London: Orion Publishing.

Dawkins, R. (ed.) (2008) *The Oxford Book of Modern Science Writing*, Oxford: Oxford University Press.

Dawkins, R. (2009) *The Greatest Show on Earth*, New York: Free Press.

Dweck, C. (2006) *Mindset: The New Psychology of Success*, New York: Ballantine Books.

Hattie, J. (2012) *Visible Learning for Teachers*, Abingdon: Routledge.

Kumar, M. (2009) *'Quantum', Einstein, Bohr and the Great Debate about the Nature of Reality*, London: Icon Books.

Okasha, S. (2002) *Philosophy of Science: A Very Short Introduction*, Oxford: Oxford University Press.

Rogers, B. (2011) *Classroom Behaviour: A Practical Guide to Effective Teaching, Behaviour Management and Colleague Support*, London: Sage.

Bibliography

Wiliam, D. (2011) *Embedded Formative Assessment*, Bloomington, IN: Solution Tree Press.

Willingham, D.T. (2009) *Why Don't Students Like School?* San Francisco, CA: Jossey-Bass.

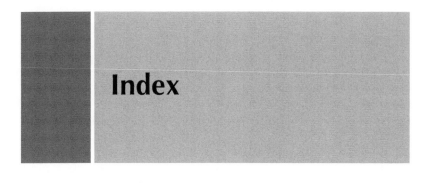

Index

accuracy and precision 26
acids and alkalis 144
analogies 115–19
animal rights 29
apparatus 146–51
Association of Science Educators
143
awe and wonder 10–11

behaviour management 12,
77–101; assertiveness 79–80;
conflict resolution 98–9;
consequences and sanctions 92–7;
group dynamics 90–2; language
87–90
Bohr model 22
Bunsen burners 144, 148

CASE, King's College 23
chemical reactions 107–8,
110–12
chemicals 150
circus experiments 163–4
CLEAPPS 143
climate change 29
Copernicus 17, 19
Cox, Brian 10
creationism 27
Curie, Marie 21

curriculum 31–50; enacted
curriculum 36–9; science
curriculum at a glance 33;
spiral curriculum 34, 48–9

Darwin, Charles 20
data 61–4
data-logging 151
Dawkins, Richard 20
debates 137–9
demonstrations 6, 141–2, 151–9
diagrams 109–14
differentiation 51–76, 107
digestion model 162–3
displacement reactions 161
Dweck, Carol 64

ecosystems 49
Einstein, Albert 18
electrical circuits 115–16, 145, 148,
168–9
electrolysis 71
emotional well-being 100
energy 43, 73, 161
energy transfers 163–4, 183
enzymes 154
evolution 20, 27, 117–18
exam questions 130–1
explaining 102–18

Index

family tree 37
Faraday, Michael 12
feedback 57; closing the gap
  marking 192–3; formative use of
  summative tests 192; oral
  feedback 186–7; written feedback
  187–90
food tests 164
food webs and food chains 43
formative assessment 177–9
fractional distillation apparatus
  151
fume cupboard 151

Galileo 18–19
gifted and talented provision
  65–7
group work 135–9
grouping strategies 72–3
growth mindset 64

Hattie, John 102
health and safety 143–6
heart cross-section 112,114
heat transfer 105–6, 117
history of science 18–22
homework 57
Hubble Ultra Deep Field image 10
Hume, David 16

investigations 160, 164–6

job applications: application forms
  199; interview lessons 203;
  interviews 200–3

kinetic theory 42
Kuhn, Thomas 17

Large Hadron Collider 22
learning objectives 56, 179–81
light 19, 49
linear air track 108
literacy 63

loudspeaker 112–13

marking see feedback
measurements 18, 24–6
metals 164
microbes 145
microscopes 149
mini-whiteboards 71, 125–7
mixed-ability groups 59
models 107–9
momentum 36, 108
multimedia products 133–4

neutralisation reactions 104–5
Newton, Sir Isaac 18
nuclear power 29–30

Okasha, Samir 16
organ dissections 145, 149
oscilloscopes 149

particles 40–3
peer and self-assessment 190–2
pendulum experiment 162
phases of the moon 110
philosophy of science 16–19
photosynthesis 43
planning 51–8
plant growth 148, 165–6
Popper, Karl 17
potential and kinetic energy 166
practical lessons 6, 159–73
practical reports 171–2
presentations 137–9
problem-solving 128–30

questioning 71; dialogic
  questioning 127; probing
  questions 119–21;
  think–pair–share 122–5

radioactive sources 21, 150
rates of reaction 36, 156–7, 165
relationships 18, 23

research notes and reports 132–3
respiration 49
risk assessments 141
Rogers, Bill 87

scale 45–7
senses 106
sex education 28
social, moral, spiritual and cultural
    education 11
solar system 18
solids, liquids and gases 116
sound 106

special educational needs 63
success criteria 179, 181–4

technicians 140–2

Van der Graaf generator 145, 150
variables 23–5
Visking tubing 109, 162

Wallace, Alfred 20
Watson and Crick 21
Wiliam, Dylan 42
writing frames 68–9